Naskapi

Mistassini

Montagnais

Abitibi

Timagami

Huron

Tête-de-Boule

Micmac

Malecite

Abenaki

Algonkin

Ojibwa

Mohawk

Ottawa

Oneida

Mississauga

Iroquois

Potawatomi

Wyandot

Onondaga

Tuscarora

Cayuga

Delaware

Seneca

Cherokee

Culture Areas, c. 1800

Northern Plains Indians

Northeastern Forest Indians

Great Lakes Indians

Huron and Iroquois

"Bo'jou, Neejee!"

Profiles of Canadian Indian Art

Bo'jou Bonjour *(French)*
Neejee Friend *(Ojibwa)*

The title of this exhibition was a common greeting throughout the Canadian north in the days of the fur trade. In the white/Indian origin of its components, its association with the fur trade and the bush, and its strong Canadian identity, the title strikingly reflects the content of this exhibition.

Cover plate

A portrait of Sir John Caldwell, fifth baronet of Castle Caldwell, County Fermanagh, Ireland. He served in North America from 1774 to 1780 as an officer in the King's Eighth Regiment of Foot, stationed at Fort Niagara and Fort Detroit. During this period he was elected chief of the Ojibwa Indians, who gave him the name Apatto, or Runner. After his return to Ireland, an unknown artist painted Caldwell dressed in Indian finery he brought back from North America. Most of these Caldwell artifacts were acquired by Arthur Speyer, Jr., and ultimately by the National Museum of Man when it bought the Speyer Collection. Many are displayed in this exhibition (Nos. 21, 32, 63, 64, 67, 77, 78, 100, 102, 103, 112, 113, 114, 117, 118, 130, 140, 147 and 173). The painting is in the collection of the King's Regiment, Merseyside County Museums, Liverpool, England.

"Bo'jou, Neejee!"

Profiles of Canadian Indian Art

Ted J. Brasser

"Bo'jou, Neejee!"

A travelling exhibition of the
National Museum of Man, Ottawa

English edition ISBN 0-660-00008-3   French edition ISBN 0-660-00009-1

Published by the
National Museum of Man
The National Museums of Canada

Published with financial assistance
from the Education and Cultural
Development Branch of the
Department of Indian and Northern
Affairs

Managing editor: Norman J. Boudreau
Staff editor: Viviane Appleton
Photography: Richard Garner and the
                Photographic Section
Design: Jacques Charette and
           Associates Ltd.
Printing: Pierre Des Marais Inc.

Available by mail from the
National Museums of Canada
Marketing Services Division
Ottawa, Ontario   K1A 0M8

Printed in Canada

Second printing

Contents

Foreword
by William E. Taylor, Jr.

"It does not seem right that such valuable space should be taken up by Esquimaux dresses, canoes, hideous feather idols, broken flints and so on", said the British Museum's greatest Victorian administrator. In those words, he expressed a commonly-held view, founded on an arrogant ethnocentrism and born of ignorance and innocence. Its rationale was based on the assumption that western European civilization of the nineteenth century represented the pinnacle of human achievement; that the classical world, the Renaissance and the Victorian age were the sources of man's greatest art. Despite the prevalence of that myth of cultural and aesthetic supremacy, there were individuals and institutions that saw the scholarly consequence and artistic merit of the products of other very different cultures. The coexistence of two such disparate viewpoints is surely understandable, for this was the feisty century of discovery that gave birth to ethnology and to modern art—an art of new concepts that was soon to borrow from the tribal art of other continents.

Leading museums in Europe and Great Britain collected ethnographical material, as did kings, dukes and private citizens. Thus did the great museums of the Old World establish major holdings of African, Oceanic, and Latin and North American artifacts. In contrast to those British officers, Swiss gentlemen, and assorted wandering artists and scientists who visited North America, the settlers largely concerned themselves with expansion, pioneering and development, rarely with preserving evidence of distinctive and rapidly changing cultures. There were few notable collections in Canada of Canadian Indian material of the early period.

This exhibition presents outstanding examples of such rare early material, pieces whose like have not existed, until recently, in our national collections. In acknowledging Canadian indebtedness to Old World museums and individuals that pursued such a legacy for us all, this note should express our particular regard for Arthur Speyer, father and son, of Eltville on the Rhine, and the Earls of Caledon in Ulster. The collections they gathered and maintained are the backbone of this exhibition. Only through their cooperation, generosity and understanding was the National Museum of Man able to repatriate the Speyer and Caledon collections as a resident part of the Canadian legacy.

Canada was offered a hard, clear lesson in the costs of cultural colonialism and ethnocentrism in the nineteenth century. Yet, to this day, it seems not to have been well learned. Still struggling with the ghost of our colonial past, confusing chauvinism with nationalism while aspiring to an international image, we often underrate our richness, variety and achievements. If Canadians are characteristically critical of their own performance, let it be remembered that an increasing number seek to achieve a better balance. A considerable range of curators and scholars have acted from a conviction of Canadian cultural worth; people like Marius Barbeau, William Notman, and Helen Creighton are far more numerous than they were fifty years ago. Moreover, there has developed a larger cadre of active, far-sighted private collectors—people like David Stewart, Walter Koerner, Eric Harvey, Robert and Signe McMichael, Henry Birks, John Langdon, Margaret Hess, Peter Winkworth, and Gerry Twomey. Having sat in a seat of government for some years, I might add that governments at various levels are more vigorously discharging their duties to preserve and transmit our traditions. Perhaps the pre-eminent government figure over the past few years has been M. Gérard Pelletier, the former Secretary of State for Canada. As ethnocentrism and self-doubt decline, cultural maturity and wider understanding increase. Hopefully then, this exhibition, a tribute to Canadian Indian cultures, will be seen in that richer perspective, and all will welcome its occupying "such valuable space".

Lenders to the Exhibition

The National Museum of Man
and the author wish to record their
appreciation to the following
institutions and individuals for
their generosity and assistance in
developing this exhibition.

Amon Carter Museum of Western
Art, Fort Worth, Texas

Art Gallery of Ontario, Toronto

Glenbow-Alberta Institute, Calgary

Hudson's Bay Company, Winnipeg

Joslyn Art Museum, Omaha, Nebraska
(Northern Natural Gas Company
Collection)

Mr. Oren R. Lyons, Nedrow,
New York

McCord Museum, Montreal

Merseyside County Museums,
Liverpool, England
(King's Regiment Collection)

National Gallery of Canada, Ottawa

National Museum of Natural Sciences,
Ottawa

Peabody Museum of Archaeology and
Ethnology, Cambridge, Massachusetts

Public Archives of Canada, Ottawa

Royal Ontario Museum, Toronto

Sœurs Grises de Montréal

West Point Museum, United States
Military Academy, West Point,
New York

Profiles of Canadian Indian Art

by Ted J. Brasser

With great pride the National Museum of Man recently announced its success in returning to Canada one of the most outstanding collections of Canadian Indian objects known to have been in private hands. Named after its former owner, Mr. Arthur Speyer, the collection consists of 259 objects made during the eighteenth and early nineteenth centuries.

Some readers may accept this information with an honest "So what?" Indeed, that question is valid, seeing that most publications of this nature take it for granted that everyone is aware of the specific nature of ethnographic museums and the function of their collections. The idea is widespread and persistent that these are simply another sort of "art" museum, where one goes to see and enjoy the aesthetic quality of peculiar objects.

The insatiable curiosity about human life in other places and other times is an ancient, yet still distinct, feature of Western society—a curiosity that made us seem distinctly odd to most other peoples. The acknowledgement that man-made objects reveal social and economic conditions has enabled us to acquire an understanding of the producers' ways of life, and has made it possible to trace the history of those societies far beyond the period of written records. The activities of museums in these respects have contributed greatly to a growing mutual understanding and respect between ethnic groups all over the world.

Pre-1850 Indian artifacts are extremely rare in ethnographic museums, where they are considered the irreplaceable treasures of the collections. Starting in the 1890s, the first Canadian Indian material arrived at the Geological Survey of Canada, for even then there was no national museum! The greater part of all North American Indian collections originated from twentieth-century native communities. As such, they document recent cultural change, but are certainly not representative of truly traditional cultures.

In contrast, many of the artifacts in the Speyer Collection were acquired during the eighteenth century, and very few were made after 1850. Their importance is obvious; traditional arts and crafts, enriched by the merchandise of the fur trade, were still vigorously alive at that time. Thus, the Speyer Collection has substantially extended the documented history of native Canadians. In combination with acquisitions of more recent origin, it enables us to study and illustrate creative developments and processes of cultural change over long periods of time. In order to show the importance of the Speyer Collection in this regard, several more-recently-made artifacts have been included in the exhibition.

It was the predominantly Canadian emphasis in the Speyer Collection that stimulated the National Museum of Man to acquire it. Most of the Canadian Indian tribes east of the Rocky Mountains are represented, plus a number of culturally related groups living across the political boundary drawn by the white man. The regions best represented are the Northern Plains, the eastern half of the Northern Forest, the Great Lakes, and the St. Lawrence drainage system, occupied by the Iroquois and Huron tribes (Map 1). Selection being a practical requirement, the exhibition will be restricted to these four regions.

Identification of the culture areas represented was made possible to a large extent by the suprising amount of documentation that Mr. Speyer managed to retrieve. This aspect in itself is one of the great merits of the collection. It is well known that most of the early artifacts that survived the ravages of war, fire, insects, exchange and time lost all written clues to their origin and history in the process. This may not reduce their attraction for the curio dealer, but it certainly does detract from their value as documents of a particular culture at a specific time. Discriminating in attitude, the former owner of the collection by preference selected those pieces which still possessed at least fragments of documentation; thus, it was possible to provide documentation for most of the artifacts in this exhibition.

Within these regional limitations, the collection presents a wide range of different techniques and artifact types. Even to the specialist this collection is an eye-opener because of the staggering variety and complexity of native arts and crafts that once existed in the Canadian wilderness. Was it perhaps precisely this harsh environment that stimulated the native artisans to call from within themselves such creative imagination, in an effort to deny human insignificance? The collection adds the urgently required "visibility" to our increasing knowledge of early native life. Rarely does one encounter objects of this age in so pristine a condition. Apparently many of the pieces were new when purchased from the Indians as souvenirs by early travellers, who never used them. However, the great age of these perishable objects has made them extremely fragile.

It is clear that a most intriguing history of European collecting activities is hidden behind all these objects. The son of an entomologist and mineralogist of Hamburg, Germany, Arthur Speyer, Sr. (1894-1958) was a born collector. Well known in German museum circles, his ethnographic collection originally included outstanding specimens from all the major areas of ethnographic art. After 1926, however, his interests focused almost exclusively on early North American Indian objects, whose rarity proved a challenge to his patience, resourcefulness and perseverance. Years of painstaking detective work in Europe resulted in the growth of the collection by both purchase and exchange. Tracing the descendants of early travellers, many of whom belonged to the German and British aristocracy, Speyer managed to save exotic heirlooms from destruction and acquired them for his collection. Several European museums owe some of their finest African and Oceanic specimens to the Speyer family, who exchanged these artifacts for North Americana, which were not always appreciated by art-oriented museum directors.

In the meantime, Arthur Speyer, Jr., had joined his father in this exciting research, which dominated their family life for many decades. Notwithstanding great difficulties—the terrors of a Nazi regime and a world war, the increasing difficulties and costs involved in locating and obtaining quality pieces—the Speyers persevered, and succeeded remarkably well in the realization of their dream. After his father's death, Arthur Speyer, Jr., found new contacts as well as entry to old private collections. Where possible, he exchanged duplicates for other specimens, but rarely found artifacts of better quality than those already in his collection. He still acquired an occasional piece at English auctions, but skyrocketing prices had become prohibitive.

Ending the many years of quiet and near-secret activity, the owner showed his collection to the public in the Deutsches Ledermuseum of Offenbach am Main during the 1968 International Congress of Americanists in West Germany (Benndorf and Speyer 1968). Speyer experienced this glorious event as the finale of a great adventure, and shortly afterwards he agreed to part with the collection.

One question remains to be answered: how did all these treasures turn up in Europe?

The phenomenon of collecting exotic curiosities is an old and distinct part of European cultural and intellectual history. Not only was the American Indian considered a symbol of everything noble and "natural" by eighteenth-century Europeans, but Indian-made artifacts became objects of marvel and contemplation during the age of exploration and colonial expansion. They led to a less prejudiced view of other peoples' achievements, enlarged the boundaries of anthropological thought, and stimulated the production of souvenirs by the Indians themselves. Nearly everyone connected with the early European exploration and settlement of the New World collected examples of native arts and crafts and sent them back to the Old Country, North America then being a frontier without museums. Even the King of France, some time after 1740, had a collection of Indian curios assembled for the entertainment of his son. Some of the artifacts in the Speyer Collection were brought back by returning German mercenaries, the Hessians employed by the British against the American revolutionaries.

For a long time the recognition of these curios as documents of distinct and different cultures remained rather vague. With no intention of "faking", the French settlers developed a souvenir industry at an early date. From about 1714 onwards, French nuns in Quebec and Montreal turned out large numbers of birch-bark trinkets, beautifully embroidered *dans le goût sauvage* with dyed porcupine quills and moose hair. Only slightly later the French Canadians started to produce woven sashes, many of which are still thought to be of Indian origin. By the early 1800s, the Huron, Iroquois and Red River Métis were manufacturing gorgeously decorated moccasins and other apparel for white customers. The increasing demand for Indian-made objects also stimulated several fur traders and military officers to devote some of their time to collecting such things with the intention of selling them when they returned to "civilization".

In the same period, a surprising number of artists explored the Indian country in search of "a setting for my Adam and Eve, a paradise that bears the character of early nature", as one of them expressed their common aspiration (Kurz 1937:90). Strange people indeed, these whites. Artists like Bodmer, Catlin, Kane, Kurz, Krieghoff and Rindisbacher left us a great many sketches and paintings, which constitute a priceless record of Indian life. The resemblance of artifacts in our collection to those shown in these early pictures is fascinating, and most instructive as to their function, origin and age. A selection of these pictures has been woven into this exhibition in order to provide context and flavour.

There were many fervent collectors among the European upper class, who compared and exchanged curios with each other as we do coins and stamps. Some of them organized expeditions to acquire the artifacts directly from the Indians, whereas others obtained their cherished pieces through acquaintances stationed in the Indian country. They created Cabinets of Curiosities, some of which have long since disappeared, but others became the first public museums during the nineteenth century. The Speyer Collection contains many artifacts formerly owned by an impressive selection of German and British nobility. Other outstanding pieces in this exhibition were obtained by the Earl of Caledon during his military service in Canada in 1841–42; his collection was acquired by the National Museum of Man in 1969. The romantic relationship felt by these noblemen with the people of Powhatan, Pontiac and Poundmaker undoubtedly contributed to the creation of the dignified Indian chief of literary and motion-picture fame. On the other hand, our conception of early native arts and crafts would have been extremely hazy without the wide-ranging interests of these collectors. It is true that many artifacts perished in Europe, but neither would they have survived all these years in Indian hands. Take, for example, the large-scale destruction of medicine bags by the Ojibwa and other followers of the prophet Tenskwatawa in 1809, or the widespread custom of burying the deceased with their most cherished possessions.

In the arrangement of this exhibition an effort has been made to let the objects tell the story of Indian ingenuity and creativity during a period in which the native societies were being caught up in rapid change. Within the period from about 1750 to 1850, two major phases of native culture overlap and can be shown separately. The first part of the exhibition concentrates on the truly aboriginal heritage: native use of the natural resources, the traditional interpretation of the natural environment, and the regional art styles of great antiquity. In the second part our focus will be upon the meeting of the native world with the European, the fascinating ways the Indian artisan selected and reinterpreted goods and ideas offered by the white man, and the distinct changes these contacts brought about in regional art styles.

It is our hope that this exhibition will spark a renewed interest in Canadian Indian history by presenting these examples of the beauty, sophistication and humanity of its legacy.

Sacred Was This Land

The Outside of Things

In the early years of our museums, the craftwork of so-called "primitive" societies was exhibited in combination with stuffed animals, minerals, and a wide range of other natural objects. The implication was clear: all those who had not yet achieved the glorified stage of farming and the blessings of Christian belief were mere phenomena of nature. To be sure, these feelings were mutual; tribal peoples frequently made it clear in the name used for their own group that outsiders had not achieved an acceptable level of humanity. Although we are no longer so complacently sure of the supreme quality of our own culture, it remains true that there was a strong and direct relationship between the natural environment and the cultures of the Indian hunters and gardeners. Most instructive in this regard was the seasonal cycle of activities in the various regions treated in this exhibition (see table).

Lacking the fruitful and continuous foreign influences that stimulated and enriched European culture, the native population of the Americas was to a large extent limited to its own ingenuity in exploiting the environment. Created during many centuries of near isolation, the Indian world becomes visible to us in the materials, tools and techniques through which the people adapted to their surroundings. Although nature posed serious limitations, almost every natural material was employed by Indian craftsmen in one way or another. Moreover, a vast network of intertribal trade relationships made possible the exchange of a wide range of goods not produced locally

Seasonal Cycle of Activities

Northern Plains

March–May	After a spring ritual the people break up their winter camps and move out into the open plains, stalking the moving buffalo and killing the calves for containers and children's robes; gathering of edible roots, making backrests, repairing dog travois, and opening the sacred-pipe bundles after the first thunder in spring.
May–June	Many small bands hunt the buffalo
June–August	Tribe unites for communal summer hunt, the annual Sun Dance and the ceremonies of various societies; the gathering of berries.
September–November	Tribe disperses again into bands, some of which occasionally unite to drive buffalo herds into pounds or over cliffs; gradual retreat to winter camps; organizing of war raids; gathering berries and firewood; making new tipi covers.
December–March	Separate winter camps, each consisting of several families, along the edge of woods or in protected river valleys, at distances of one or two days' journey from one another; craftwork, storytelling period; some hunting.

Northeastern Forest

February–April	Having left their winter camps, the people wander about hunting moose and caribou and ice-fishing; but there are frequent periods of starvation.
April	Return to canoe caches at previous fall camps; fishing.
April–May	Hunting of waterfowl, muskrat, otter; fishing; gathering cranberries; spring feast.
May–June	Return to summer camp of band.
June–August	Band is together at summer camp; feasting, fishing, picking berries, gathering bark for manufacture of canoes and containers.
September	Families leave summer camp in groups; hunting of ducks and muskrats; fishing.
September–October	Hunting of moose, caribou and bear; fishing; gathering berries; fall feast.
October–November	Hunting groups establish separate winter camps; gathering of firewood; construction of supply caches, snowshoes, toboggans, snowshovels; winter ritual.
November–December	Trapping of furbearing animals (post-contact period).
January	Midwinter feast; breakup of winter camps to pursue caribou and moose.

Great Lakes

March–April	People camp in maple groves to tap trees for syrup and to make sugar; gathering of inner bark of cedar for manufacture of bags; ice-fishing.
April	Some plant corn, beans and squash; others go on trading expeditions; fishing; hunting of small game.
May	Major fishing period; gathering of birds' eggs, wild roots and berries; gardeners work in their fields.

June–August	Gathering of rushes and inner-bark fibres to make bags and mats; gathering of bark for baskets and canoes; gathering of hickory for making arrows; fishing; gardeners work in their fields.
September	Harvesting wild rice, cultivated corn, etc.; hunting pigeons.
October	Fishing.
November	Band leaves summer camp; families move to their separate hunting grounds.
December–March	Band dispersed, families living in winter camps; making of snowshoes; hunting; ice-fishing.

Huron and Iroquois

March	Hunting of moose.
April	Families camp in and exploit sugar bush; Maple Ritual; gathering firewood; hunting passenger pigeons; fishing.
May	Burning and clearing of garden fields; Planting Ritual and planting of corn; gathering wild fruits; fishing; relocation of village every 8 to 12 years.
June	Strawberry Ritual; gathering of wild fruits; working in gardens; fishing; repairing bark houses and stockades; manufacturing bark containers and canoes.
July	Green Corn Ritual; working in gardens; gathering wild fruits.
August	Harvest Ritual; harvesting and storing corn, beans and squashes.
September	Harvesting, hunting and fishing; organizing war raids.
October	Communal deer drives; fishing; war raids.
November	Hunting and fishing.
December	People return from fishing and hunting camps to main village.
December–March	People live off summer supplies in main village; Midwinter Ritual; nightly meeting of medicine societies; craftwork; some ice-fishing.

Animal skins rank first in any enumeration of materials used by the Canadian Indians. Fresh, tanned or smoked, skins were used to cover the bodies as well as the dwellings of the people, who converted smaller skins into a variety of bags
*1 and pouches, or cut up the fresh skins into rawhide thongs. Such thongs were
3 used wet for webbing snowshoes, tying stone celts to wooden handles, or mending broken articles; the strings shrank as they dried and became as strong
4 as iron bands. In order to make an animal skin suitable for clothing, remaining meat particles and the tissue under the skin were first scraped off; then preserving substances were rubbed in to make the skin soft and pliable. Among the Woodland Indians particularly, smoking of the skin might come next, which guarded it against rot and kept it pliable. Many groups also rubbed skin clothing and utensils with red ochre to prevent them from stiffening after being wet. The soft skins of the antique specimens in museum collections testify to the unsurpassed quality of the Indian tanning methods. Our modern techniques demand less work and time, but do not yield such a durable product.

Next in importance to animal skins was bark, the skin of trees. The bark of the paper birch in the northern forest and that of the elm farther south was carefully peeled from the trees in large sheets and was used to cover the frames of
5 wigwams and canoes. Boxes, baskets, spoons, mats, masks, rattles and a variety of other utensils were made of bark. Whereas the Plains Indians wrapped their dead in large skins, the Woodlands Indians buried theirs wrapped in bark. There are many other parallels between the use of the skin of trees by Canadian forest Indians and that of animals by the Indians of the virtually treeless western plains. To a large extent this also applies to the regional use of bone and wood. Another intriguing correlation is apparent between manufactures of bark and skin. Whereas the bark of trees was invariably sewn with split roots, animal skin was sewn with shredded sinew. Does a rational explanation in terms of regional adaptation and the nature of the materials suffice? After all, sinew was used all over the country for sewing skins, and bark was used to some extent on the northern plains. Religious beliefs, as existed in the seasonal switch from sea to land exploitation among the Eskimos, may have played a role in the bark-root and skin-sinew correlations among the Indians. Was it considered offensive to the forest spirits to sew bark with a material given by the animal spirits, and vice versa?

Generally, awls were made of bone, and needles from long thorns. Sinew thread has the advantage of swelling when wet, thus helping to keep footwear waterproof.

6 Bullrushes, basswood-bark fibre, nettle-stalk fibre, Indian hemp and several other fibres, as well as buffalo wool were used around the Great Lakes in the weaving and twining of mats, bags, nets, burden straps and sashes.

Wood, bone and stone come next in our list of native materials. Obviously, the use of wood was well developed among the Indians in the eastern forests.
8 Specially selected types of wood were worked into bows and arrows, war clubs, snowshoes, toboggans, canoe frames and paddles, bowls and spoons, pipe stems, flutes, drums, masks, and many other items. These were made by charring, scraping, and cutting with beaver teeth or flints set in wooden handles or with shells and other tools made of stone, bone and antler. Horns of the buffalo and
10 mountain sheep were used by the Plains Indians to make spoons, bowls and strong bows. Skin-scrapers and other tools were frequently made of bone. Soapstone, catlinite and slate were the most popular types of stone used in the carving of pipe bowls and small charms, whereas flint was worked into arrow heads by means of antler pressure-tools and hammerstones. Occasionally a highly valued copper tool was obtained; their manufacture dates from long ago in the region of Lake Superior.

*The numbers in the margin refer to artifacts illustrated in the catalogue.

11 Tempered with crushed stone, sand or shell, clay was used in the manufacture of pots and pipes (without the use of the wheel for shaping), and baked in smothered fires. Contrary to common belief, pottery was also made and used by nomadic groups.

It has often been assumed that societies based upon hunting, fishing and gathering were restricted to a mere survival level of technological development simply because the people lacked the time to refine their way of life. However, a closer look at most of these societies shows this assumption to be incorrect. It is debatable whether modern industrial society leaves more leisure time or provides more creative incentive than were formerly enjoyed by the Canadian Indians. They invented a baffling range of complex decorative techniques, utilizing a plethora of materials offered by their environment.

Earth, plants and animals provided pigments for dyeing and painting. Native place names often referred to pigments obtained there from rocks or vegetation. Other pigments might be obtained through intertribal trade. In the early years of the eighteenth century, the Blackfoot were reported to have employed at least ten different colours "in painting and daubing their garments, bodies and faces" (Henry and Thompson 1897, vol. 2 : 731). Mixed with water, grease or fish roe,

12-16 the paint was applied by means of pointed sticks, pieces of porous bone, sharp-edged antler tools, crude wooden brushes, or the artist's fingers. Designs were painted on the human body as well as on huge rocks, on the skin and bark

17 covers of tipis and wigwams, and on skin clothing, snowshoes and utensils.
18 Geometric designs on animal skins often were first outlined with heavy pressure from a heated bone tool shaped like a dull-bladed knife.

Skins, native textiles, porcupine quills and moose hair were dyed by soaking and boiling them in water mixed with plant substances and an iron-holding clay.

19 Particularly around the Great Lakes, the Indians used to dye their bags, moccasins, and other skin apparel a brownish black by means of a tannic acid derived from the bark of the walnut tree. In the same area, a kind of resist- or discharge-

21 dye technique was used on finger-braided bags and sashes.

22 Used as the outside of containers, the brown inside surface of birch bark lent itself to decoration by means of scraped patterns. The same technique was occasionally employed on rawhide containers by the Eastern Sioux, Blackfoot and some tribes on the Central Plains.

23-28 Unique to the North American Indians was the use of coloured porcupine quills in the decoration of skin and bark. Nowhere else has this art form been recorded, although it may be related to a similar use of reindeer hair in Greenland, Alaska and Siberia. The quills were used in four principal techniques: wrapping, sewing, plaiting and weaving. Tribes living outside the range of the porcupine obtained quills in trade, although sometimes substitutes were used, such as split bird-quills and vegetable fibres. The Cree bands of the northern forest used coloured moose hair to embroider skin objects. The Huron and

29 Iroquois employed it to create geometric designs by wrapping the hairs around the weft of twined woven bags and straps in a technique called "false embroidery".

Mention has been made above of wood and stone carving, in which the Huron and Iroquois, in particular, excelled. Although we know very little about the quality of their mask carving before the introduction of European steel tools, effigy pipes of clay, wood and stone testify to a highly developed craftsmanship. Beaver-shaped wooden bowls in the Great Lakes region and buffalo effigies found on the northwestern Plains indicate that the Indians there were also skilled in three-dimensional sculpture.

31 Extensive use was made of feathers, tassels of dyed hair, quill-wrapped and netted fringes, the dewclaws of deer for jinglers, bear and bird claws for necklaces, and seeds, shells, stones and native copper as beads. Exotic raw materials were eagerly sought for their prestige value. As a rule, however, the native artist used whatever material was most readily available; his aim was good craftsmanship.

As in most pre-industrial societies, a traditional division of labour and craftwork by sex was maintained, providing everyone with a source of prestige and satisfaction. Women prepared skins and made clothing, tipi covers, and rawhide, bark and ceramic containers. They did all the weaving, quillwork, snowshoe webbing and conventional geometric painting. It is obvious that a large proportion of the artifacts in this exhibition were made by women. Men produced equipment for the hunt, war, and ceremonial activities. They carved bowls, spoons, snowshoe frames, paddles, pipes, masks and cradleboards, painted realistic and symbolic pictures on tipi covers, robes, shields, drums and rock surfaces, and constructed longhouses, stockades, wigwams, canoes, toboggans and travois. While each family could produce almost everything necessary for its survival, certain individuals were known for their exceptional ability in a specific craft. Outstanding quillworkers were united in professional guilds among the Cheyenne and perhaps among the Blackfoot and other tribes as well. It has been suggested that polygamous marriages among the Naskapi arose out of the religious requirement for producing several painted-skin coats annually for each man; a hunter needed an extra wife to do all the intricate painting. Even for such specialists, however, artistic production was not a permanent or exclusive occupation.

The Dream Pictured

Instead of explaining the subject of this exhibition personally to each visitor, I have undertaken to write down the information in this book. Quite simple, but behind this act stretches the thousands of years it took to catch and preserve the sound of language in writing. In the course of this development, man went through a series of experiments ranging from pictographs to the abstract sound-symbols of our own script. However, whether a smoke signal or the Morse alphabet, memorized knowledge of its code is essential for reading the message.

33 The Iroquois and their neighbours used belts woven of white and purple shell-beads, called "wampum", to convey important messages. Wampum was selected for this purpose because of its ancient connotations of sacredness and prestige. The importance attached to the wampum belt is indicated by the fact that an oral message required the confirmation provided by such a belt to be accepted as truth. Thus, the belt was called the "mouth" of the individual or group who sent the message. One of the tribal chiefs was appointed as Keeper of the Wampum; he took care of the tribal archives of wampum belts and strings, and he memorized the messages that had been "talked" into them. When required during important occasions, this official would show the old belts and recount their meanings.

Nobody can retrieve the exact message symbolized by a particular belt once its meaning is lost. In general, we know that belts with a white background indicated peace, health, well-being and prosperity, whereas the predominantly purple belts referred to hostility, sorrow, death, condolence and mourning. Long horizontal lines indicated trails or unions between distant nations, the latter symbolized by squares, diamonds or human figures. Diagonal lines are said to have referred to allies or to support given to the message by someone else.

When used as a declaration of war, a wampum belt was completely painted
red. Most of the old wampum belts now in museums have long since lost their
precise meaning, and the documentation as to their tribal origin is questionable.
It should be remembered that a belt collected, say, among the Ottawa was
probably received previously from somewhere else.

The use of painted or carved sticks was widespread and may predate the use of
wampum belts to record messages. The recounting of old traditions and prayers
by means of bundles of sticks during council meetings has frequently been
observed among the Indians along the Atlantic coast as well as in the region of
34 the Great Lakes. Sticks, boards and sheets of birch bark engraved with
mnemonic symbols were used by members of the Midaywiwin and other
medicine societies of the Great Lakes Indians to memorize secret prayers, songs
and medicine recipes. Even as far west as among the Alberta Blackfoot, some
ancient medicine bundles contained sets of sticks to keep count of the time by
means of lunar cycles. In contrast, historical awareness was least developed
among the hunters in the Northern Forest, where the remote Naskapi felt that
"from great-grandparents to great-grandchildren we are only knots in a string"
(Speck 1935: 236).

Whereas most of the communication systems were understood only by the
initiated, pictographic drawings on tipi covers and on the inside of longhouses
proclaimed the impressive war records of their owners for everyone to behold.
From the Iroquois in the East to the Plains Indians in the West, every man was
expected to be a warrior as well as a hunter. Prolonged blood feuds led to a state
of continual conflict, offering the opportunity to win honour and social prestige
in the dangerous game of war. The development of tribal cohesion among bands
or villages appears to have been directly related to the regional importance of
warfare. Warfare with ancient ritual overtones was chronic among the Iroquois
and Huron, who developed supratribal confederacies. In contrast, warfare
among the loosely organized and independent bands of the Northeastern Forest
was restricted to occasional brawls, particularly with Eskimo neighbours on the
coast.

36 The warrior painted the story of his war exploits on his skin robe and shirt,
35 engraved it on his war clubs, and, utilizing a complex system of more-abstract
symbols, announced his prowess in the decoration of leggings, moccasins and
headdresses. Stripes painted on the leggings and shirts of Plains Indians referred
to the number of enemies touched in battle. Spots painted on the warrior's body
and on his shirt represented wounds received in battle, and a red hand painted
or quillworked on a Sioux warrior's dress showed that he had killed an enemy
in hand-to-hand combat. Modesty was indeed rare in the context of warfare.

37 Only the most prominent warriors were entitled to wear the scalp shirt. The
making of such a shirt was a ritual event participated in by invited comrades,
who each contributed scalp locks to the decoration of the shirt. A group of
warrior comrades also used to combine their war records in the paintings on
buffalo robes or tipi covers and in the construction of large headdresses of eagle
feathers. Among the Plains and the Great Lakes Indians, each eagle feather represented a particular war-deed, its precise nature indicated by how the feather
was decorated. The crown of feathers was represented by the Feathered Circle
design, painted or quillworked on skin robes by the Indians of the Central
Plains. Both headdress and design symbolized the Sun, the great warrior in
mythology. In his honour the Iroquois sacrificed their prisoners after cruel
torture.

38 A fascinating example of oral history has been handed down with the impressive headdress in this exhibition. According to this tradition, the headdress once belonged to Chief Little Crow (1803-1863), who led the Eastern Sioux in their war against the Minnesota settlers in 1862. As a result of this war, many of these Indians fled to Canada, where they settled in Manitoba and Saskatchewan. In 1851, however, Little Crow had given this headdress as a gift to a Sisseton Sioux chief, and it was worn by Chief Rain-in-the-Face in the Battle of the Little Bighorn in 1876, where General Custer met his defeat. Besides the long trailer of eagle feathers, the headdress is decorated with a pair of deer antlers, introducing a vast and complex body of religious symbolism.

Behind the bewildering variety of myths and rituals, each distinctive to certain tribes, a few basic concepts of religious thought are discernible that were understood throughout the greater part of Indian North America. Fundamental to the native interpretation of the environment was the belief that animals, rocks and all other natural phenomena possessed spiritual power. In their world interpretation there was no coincidence; everything had its deeper meaning. Having long since deprived our reality of much of its spiritual dimension, we call such an invisible asset "supernatural", but to the Indian this power was completely real and natural. Through it the world was sanctified, and all interrelationships between man, the animals, the rivers, the forest and the sky were sacred. Their sacred nature was expressed in numerous ritual practices, none of them spectacular but performed every day. The Indian strongly believed that it was this consecration of everyday work that produced the desired results and the well-being of the people. This was considered particularly true in hunting and fishing; that is, man was dependent upon the goodwill of the animal spirits.

All animals were thought to be grouped in tribes of their own kind, their chiefs standing in hierarchical relation to each other. If treated in the right way, the spirits of slain animals would be reincarnated. Similar ideas were entertained with regard to plants, particularly by the gardening tribes. Those along the Missouri River were convinced that every plant had its own song, and the Three Sisters—corn, beans and squash—were respected spirits among the Iroquoians.

Central to the ritual techniques for contacting and manipulating the forces of nature was the dream, or "vision". A man in search of sacred power went to a lonely spot, where he fasted and prayed until he met a spiritual guardian in a dream. There is timeless and universal truth in the native belief that true wisdom is to be found far from human society, out in the wilderness, and that it can be acquired only by suffering. Privation and suffering can open a man's mind to what is hidden from others. Through the study and interpretation of his dreams, man cultivated an intense communication with his spiritual guardian. In exchange, he acquired dream songs, symbolic art designs, and instruction in the art of curing, in weather control or in the construction of protective paraphernalia. Seeking to strengthen his relationship with the spirits, a man would frequently concentrate his thoughts and willpower by singing dream songs,

39 beating a drum, or smoking his pipe. Effigies carved on these pipes were popular among the Iroquoians and in the Great Lakes region. Directed towards the smoker, they represented his guardian spirit. Tobacco smoke was regarded as an incense beloved of the spirits and possessing mediatory powers with them.

Although the rituals acquired in this way were frequently performed upon request for the benefit of others, the exact nature of the spiritual experience and the meaning of vision-derived symbols were to be kept secret in order to maintain their effect. Ancient and worldwide was the idea that words are vehicles of power that can be transferred from speaker to receiver: "In the beginning was the Word, and the Word was God". However, certain paraphernalia or decorative designs were generally understood to refer to the owner's vision

40 power. Wearing an ornately decorated animal skin, the Indian personified its spirit, his guardian; in songs and dances he would grunt like the bear, bellow

41 like the buffalo, howl like the wolf. Antlers in a headdress or deer feet made into moccasins referred to the sacred power acquired from a deer spirit; swiftness and agility may have been his gifts. The vision-derived paintings and other

42 decorations on a shield were normally kept hidden under a cover, only to be taken off in battle. These decorations, not the thickness of the shield, were thought to protect the warrior.

The "self-directed" character of pipe decorations referred to above is also

43 evident in the ornaments painted or embroidered on moccasins. Both naturalistic and abstract designs are meant to be looked at from the wearer's angle of view. This approach contrasts with our own, which is primarily to please the onlooker; that is, the patterns are placed upside-down from the wearer's point of view. Explicit information from many tribes, both in the eastern Woodlands and on the Plains, confirms the association of these moccasin decorations with their owners' visions. The spiritual power of such moccasins was reflected in the Sioux warriors' custom of placing their worn-out footwear on the trail with the request that they return home by themselves.

44 A similar spiritual power was believed to be present in snowshoes. The term for snowshoe is an animate one in Algonkian languages, whereas the names of most other objects are inanimate. The openwork designs in the webbing, the tassels around the frame, and the painted designs on the snowshoe had a protective function. Vicious spirits manipulated by evil conjurers were repelled by such

45-46 decorations. Painted or quillwork stripes crossing the soles of moccasins had the same protective function. However, the more elaborate decorations on moccasin soles among the Plains Indians, though derived from the old protection idea, reflected the regional focus on social prestige. Such moccasins were made for a "favourite" child of a respectable family.

The colourful paintings on the skin clothing of hunters in the Northeastern Forest were also protection against evil cannibalistic spirits. At the same time, these paintings referred to the sacred nature of hunting; the Lord of the Caribou and the animal spirits in general were pleased to see the paintings, and blessed the hunter. Evidence from the Great Lakes and the Plains regions reveals the great age and wide diffusion of this idea.

The belief that spirits inhabited rocks and stones was universal. The tribal names of the Oneida Iroquois and the Mistassini Montagnais both refer to a sacred rock in the territory of each. Throughout the vast territory of the Cree-speaking bands there are numerous sacred rocks, and even today tobacco is sometimes offered on or near many of them. Lone glacial boulders on the high plains were believed to have walked down from the mountains long ago; powerful visions were given to Blackfoot Indians who fasted and prayed near such rocks.

47 The Plains Indians believed that a strong relationship existed between these sacred rocks and the buffalo spirits. The Lord of the Buffalo Spirits himself resided in a huge boulder on Ribstone Hill in Alberta; all other sacred rocks were believed to be its descendants. Marine fossils and other oddly shaped stones were used as magical charms by the Blackfoot. Set in wads of buffalo wool, these "buffalo stones" were placed in front of the shaman, who rubbed them with red paint while he "called" the buffalo. The stones were believed to be alive: they grew, produced offspring in the shape of smaller stones and, like the buffalo, grew heavy in summertime. Although more elaborately decorated than the buffalo stones of the Blackfoot, the sacred stones of the Crow Indians figured in the same spiritual context. Not surprisingly, the buffalo loomed large in the symbolism of the Plains Indian hunters.

48 The caribou was as vitally important in the Northeastern Forest as the buffalo was on the Plains. The Naskapi, in particular, have left us rich evidence of caribou symbolism in their skin paintings. The most impressive example known to me is in the Speyer Collection: a unique painting on a nearly square sheet of caribou skin, dating back to about 1740. The white of the skin itself associates the ideas of snow, winter and caribou. The major patterns were outlined with fish glue, which has turned yellow with age. The designs were painted with the sacred colour red and with a bluish green. Basically, the surface is divided into three rectangular sections, linked together by a cross extending across the whole skin. All other details are grouped together in, and are clearly associated with, the three sections underlying the cross. The two outer sections are filled with highly conventionalized interpretations of trees and plants, presumably symbolizing the forest and summer. The central section is filled with symbols of caribou antlers, referring to the caribou herd and winter. Parallel lines and rows of dots, representing the trails and tracks of animals, surround the pictures. The total composition can be interpreted as a most impressive picture of the world, in time and space, as envisioned by the hunters of the Northeastern Forest: caribou herd versus forest, the importance of the winter hunting period in the annual cycle of seasons.

The spiritual nature of this world conception is indicated by the cross that extends across the whole composition. A Naskapi shaman had a similar design painted on his tent and drum. This cross is clearly the most important design unit, representing in a very elaborate form a well-known pattern associated with a series of widespread ideas of central importance in the native ideology. Although it was the symbol of the Soul-Spirit, the Four World-Directions, and several other regional interpretations, the cross essentially symbolized the omnipresent God—the Great Spirit—not in his remote and inactive position at the top of the cosmological pantheon, but as the Earthmaker. His representative, the Sun, is indicated by the circle at the centre of the cross; good weather was required for the caribou hunt.

The borders of the skin are trimmed with a short, quill-wrapped fringe, and hair tassels in conical brass jingles are attached to the four corners. Tassels and fringes, which were used to decorate most objects made of skin, were believed to bring success in hunting.

49 Usually overlooked is the decoration of the four corners of skins, amulets, pouches, and other containers; yet such elaboration frequently appears on objects intended for ritual use. It seems that such decorations represented the four legs of an animal, implying an animal symbolism for the whole object. This ancient symbolism extended far beyond the Northeastern Forest. The Naskapi tobacco pouch with four tabs at the bottom is strikingly similar to such pouches among the western Sioux; the opening of such a pouch was seen as the animal's mouth. Animal-shaped wooden bowls carved in the regions of the Great Lakes and the Pacific and in northwestern Russia present in visual form an associative train of thought perhaps once common to us all.

It will be clear that the Naskapi skin discussed above was intended for ritual use. We know very little about these rituals, confined as they were to the interior of the boreal forest. According to information recently obtained by Mrs. Alika Podolinsky-Webber, shamans used to wear such skins around their shoulders while luring a caribou herd to a water crossing. By means of the magic paintings on the skin, the shaman could turn himself into a caribou. Once the game had entered the crossing the shaman would reveal himself as a man, and wave his magic robe while hunters in canoes surrounded the caribou. During certain celebrations such painted skins were hung outside the lodge, the paintings facing the sun, to please the spirits and absorb new power. At all other times, however, the owner would keep the magic paintings hidden from view. Even when he used the robe for luring caribou, he wore it with the painted designs inside.

The harsh environment, the small size of the hunting bands, and their loose organization did not favour the development of communal rituals in the Northeastern Forest. Originating in visions, religious practice remained largely an individual concern. The difference between shamans and other hunters depended mainly upon the degree of spiritual power derived from vision experiences.

Although based upon the same type of experiences, complex communal rituals characterized religious life in the larger and well-organized tribes around the Great Lakes and on the Plains. Ritual leaders, or priests, were responsible for the development of a rich and detailed interpretation of the universe. Many concepts in this cosmological structure originated in ancient civilizations in the lower Mississippi region, if not from still farther south. Symbolic designs on prehistoric artifacts from these cultural centres lived on in the religious art of the historic Indian tribes, though it should not be implied that they still carried the same symbolic connotations. There is strong evidence that, in the course of centuries, mythological worlds emerged and disintegrated, and that new worlds were built from old fragments in new configurations. Of course, this can be said of all religions, related as they are to the continuous reintegration of sociopolitical entities. In the course of these developments many art designs either lost their original symbolism, disappeared, lived on as purely decorative art, or acquired new meanings.

A basically identical interpretation of the universe was shared by the tribes around the Great Lakes and those on the Plains; though seemingly divergent, the beliefs of the Iroquoian tribes were also based upon this common structure. The earth was believed to be an island, usually carried on the back of a huge turtle. Floating in an unlimited and dark ocean, this island separated the two halves of the universe into upper and lower portions. Each portion was divided into four superimposed layers, inhabited by spiritual beings whose power increased in ratio to their remoteness from the earth. Rooted in the lowest layer of the Underwater World, a huge tree grew through the centre of the earth, with its top reaching the highest layer of the Sky World. Perhaps here is an ancient common heritage, because this cosmic tree—the Tree of Life, centre-pole of the world—may well be the same one that stood in the centre of the biblical Paradise. Known as the Ever-growing Tree, it was used by the Iroquois as a symbol of their intertribal confederacy. Earth and cosmic tree together formed the cross design met with above, but here it is in its vertical position.

The spirits, or "persons", of the Sky World were antagonistic towards those of the Underwater World, but the opposition of good and evil spirits was unknown among the Indians before Christian beliefs made their impact. In the highest layer of the Sky World the Great Spirit resided, represented by the sun. Beneath him, in descending order, were three layers inhabited by the Morning Star and the Thunderers, then the Thunderbirds and, finally, lower birds of warlike character. In the third group, in addition to what we consider birds of prey, the Indians included the swallow, the woodpecker and various other birds. Throwers of lightning in their war with the Underwater beings, the Thunderers were associated with male aggression, rain and fertility.

In the lowest layer beneath the earth resided the Great Naked Bear, Lord of the Underwater World and patron of the most powerful medicine men. Next, in ascending order, were the Horned Panther (represented on earth by the lynx and the salamander), the White Deer or Caribou and, close to the surface of the earth, the Horned Hairy Snake. The spiritual masters of buffaloes, otters, beavers, reptiles, fishes and several other animals also inhabited the Underwater World. The recognition of Windmaker as an Underwater person by the Blackfoot is clearly related to the Great Lakes Indian belief that storms were caused by the Horned Panther, who lashed the waves with his long tail. The Underwater beings were primarily associated with the female aspect, herbal knowl-

50 edge and witchcraft. As decorations on Iroquoian pipes, long-tailed water animals may represent the guardian spirits of medicine men, whose curing rituals played an important role in these tribes. Assistance offered by these

51 spirits in war is reflected in the appearance of long-tailed animals carved on war clubs.

The cosmic war between the Sky and Underwater spirits can be explained as a competition for the allegiance of human beings. Each side had great powers to offer, but man had to make the choice; no one could safely have it both ways. Most of the artifacts in this part of the exhibition relate to the spirits in this pantheon. Several of these objects are associated with "medicine bundles", that is, bags or bundles containing one or more sacred objects said to have been given in visions to individuals in the legendary past. Considered to be effective, they survived as ritual instruments in public ceremonials. Among the Aztecs of Mexico, such bundles were called "the heart of the town", a description that aptly transmits the emotional feelings in North America as well concerning these tribal shrines.

52 As a counterpart to the Naskapi skin-painting, the exhibition displays a rare painted deerskin, used as the inner wrapping of a war bundle by the Menomini Indians in the region of the Great Lakes. Given by the Sky beings long ago, the picture shows their world from three different angles, surrounding or actually hovering above the ritual lodge. At one end of the skin (to the left in the photograph), the Sky World is delineated in its four successive layers. Surrounding the red rectangle, only the lowest stratum of the Sky World is shown, inhabited by warlike birds and a host of other Sky beings within reach of man's world. The third angle refers to a horizontal interpretation of the Sky World: the Thunderbirds in the west and the Sun in the east, pictured on a corner in a square house of sunshine. The visionary and protégé of the Thunderers, himself pictured as a Thunderbird, is shown in the red rectangle in the centre. This rectangle represents both the lodge in which the war-bundle ritual was performed and the earth. The symbol of the earth as a ritual lodge was a widespread concept in North America. Such a lodge or temple was always entered from the east, as indicated here by two spirits in human shape.

When addressing the Thunderbirds in prayer, the Indians around the Great
53 Lakes used to shake a rattle consisting of a bunch of deer dewclaws tied to a
stick. A Thunderbird, either in full or represented by the head only, was carved
on top of the stick. Frequently carved in a zigzag shape, the handle represented
lightning, used by the Thunderers to kill Underwater spirits. The sound
produced by the rattle symbolized the thunder. The Ojibwa conjurer protected
by the Thunderers had deer dewclaws attached to one of his lodge poles; they
would rattle when spirits entered the lodge during a seance.

Cradleboards of the western Ojibwa, Eastern Sioux, and various other tribes
around the western Great Lakes were decorated with straps of elaborate quill-
54 work. The strap in this exhibition is decorated with figures of Thunderbirds and
with zigzag lines representing lightning shooting from their eyes. Thunderbirds
were said to travel in pairs; their black colour refers to the dark clouds in which
they travel. The diamond pattern on their breasts represents their "lifeline",
indicating the spiritual nature of the birds. The long fringes below the Thunderbirds may well symbolize the rain and fertility brought by these spirits.

The symbolism associated with the Sky powers played an important role in
communal ceremonials developed around the ritual use of pipes. There is strong
evidence that a late prehistoric cult, centred in the middle Mississippi region,
was at the root of the Calumet Dance among the historic tribes of the Plains and
the Great Lakes. In both the Southeastern Cult and the Calumet Dance, bird
spirits were honoured, but whereas the former ritualized war and human sacri-
fice, the latter was performed to create friendship and make peace. War and
peace were two facets of the aggressive aspect associated with the Sky powers;
peace on earth resulted from their cosmic war against the Underwater spirits.
55 Two long pipe stems, one associated with war, the other with peace, figure in the
Calumet Dance. Decorated with the skins and feathers of birds, these pipe stems
were moved as if they were flying birds, and the same idea was mimed in the
postures of those who danced with the calumets during the ritual. The ceremony
was never held in winter, as it was addressed to the Thunderers, who were
thought to reign during the summer.

Creating sacred kinship relationships between tribes, the Calumet Dance spread
from the southern Plains to as far north as the Cree, and eastwards through the
Great Lakes region to the Iroquois. The ritual appears to have originated among
the Pawnee about 1660, and it reached the Abenaki on the St. Lawrence River in
the 1720s. The "Peace Pipe" of our literature is but a poor echo of this elaborate
complex of symbolism.

In the course of its continental wanderings, the Calumet Dance was adapted by
each tribe to fit the local version of the common religious pattern. An extreme
example of this development was the sacred Thunder Pipe Bundle among the
Blackfoot and other tribes on the Northern Plains. It is possible that the earlier
northward diffusion of the prehistoric Southeastern Cult contributed to the
divergent character of the Thunder Pipe Bundle. Whatever their precise origin
may have been, it is certain that foreign ideas were adopted selectively and
changed to fit the regional complex of sacred bundles, which originated from
individual visions.

Instead of as a means to create kinship and peace, the Thunder Pipe was used in
war rituals and to assure protection in general. Announcing the return of the
Thunderbirds, the bundle was ritually opened after the first thunder in spring.
The antagonism of the Thunderbirds towards the Underwater persons was
emphasized in various parts of the ritual. Both the robe worn by the bundle
56 keeper and the drums used in the ritual were painted with a design showing
Thunderbird claws and hail coming from a dark sky with lightning.

The impact made by the Thunder Pipe upon the religious life of the Blackfoot is indicated by their belief that this was the first sacred pipe ever given by the spirits. This belief, however, was contested by the keepers of the Beaver bundles, associated as these were with ancient myths and rituals. Yet the symbolic association of ritual pipes with the Thunderbirds was widespread.

57 Ranging from naturalistic bird designs to hourglass-shaped symbols, Thunderbirds decorated the pipe stems of the Sioux, the Ojibwa and many other tribes.

58 Closely associated with the Thunderbirds were the red Pileated and Ivory-billed woodpeckers, used to decorate pipe stems and various types of headdresses. Their association with the warlike bird spirits was based upon a series of native ideas: the woodpecker knows how to find its prey without seeing it (under the bark of trees); powerfully, the bird bores a hole within a short time; the shrill cries of the woodpecker are heard when a storm is approaching, the sound being like that of the eagle-bone whistles used in the Sun Dance; and when the bird is angry its crest rises like the roach headdress of a warrior. Opening-up-the-Clouds was the mythical name for the woodpecker among the Ojibwa, clearly associating the bird with the Sky warriors. Its role in the war against the water monsters and in the protection of man is recounted in the Glooskap myths of the Abenaki; as the "crested bird" it was the patron of Creek warriors in the southeastern United States.

The study of early ethnographic collections frequently adds colourful detail to early descriptions of native customs. Sometimes it clarifies these reports, particularly those which go into technical details. Rarely, however, do such artifacts lead us on the track of a cultural institution of which there is hardly a clue in the early reports. Such may be the case with the following group of intriguing objects.

59-60 A distinct type of black or dark-brown nearly square skin pouch is present in several old collections; about forty of them have been traced so far. These pouches were decorated with quillworked figures of Thunderbirds, Horned Underwater Panthers, or Underwater Snakes. They were made and used primarily by the Ottawa and Mississauga, but the Eastern Ojibwa, Potawatomi, Menomini, Miami and Eastern Sioux were also part of this complex. The pouches appear to have been particularly popular during the second half of the eighteenth century. The religious symbolism of their decoration, the surprisingly large number that survived, and their origin in a group of neighbouring tribes strongly suggest that they played a role in a ritual complex shared by these tribes. Apparently the pouches were used as the distinctive paraphernalia of the individual followers of this ritual or religious organization. Their decoration with figures of either Sky beings or Underwater spirits suggests that the members of this organization were divided into two groups in ritual opposition to each other.

The paraphernalia of this ritual complex, or organization, appears to have included a number of other objects closely related to the pouches in their material, style of decoration, regional origin and age. Three ritual skin mats have been found in American museums; two of them show the Sky World divided in its layers, while the third one shows the Underwater Panthers surrounded by Thunderbird symbols. There exist also a few black skin pouches cut in the shape of otter skins, and another in the shape of a turtle, all of them decorated with quillwork in the same style as on the objects mentioned above. Also closely related are some long black bags with two leg-shaped extremities at the bottom.

Beyond the general conclusions mentioned above, the interpretation of this group of related artifacts is a complex one, based upon a large body of fragmentary data that require more study. In summary it would appear that a cult, probably called the Black Dance, emerged in the region of the eastern Great Lakes about the middle of the eighteenth century. The mythological beliefs and shamanistic practices incorporated in this cult were very similar to those of the Midaywiwin, a religious society that emerged among the Wisconsin Ojibwa at about the same time or slightly later. Whereas the latter spread among several tribes and is well known because of its survival to the present, the Black Dance Society had a rather short life, and is hardly mentioned in the early records. There is evidence that the Black Dance ritual was concerned with hunting and war, reflecting the fur trade and colonial wars, in which its followers played an important role. In contrast, the activities of the Midaywiwin focused upon the magical curing of the sick and, through preservation of the tribal traditions, supported the integration and cultural unification of the widespread Ojibwa
61 bands. The members of the Midaywiwin carried otter and other animal skins as containers for their sacred medicines.

The masks used in curing ceremonies by the Iroquois reflect the different world view of these gardeners. Their world was not one shared with the spirits of nature; it was the village surrounded by its gardens—the humanized clearing in the forest. The surrounding wilderness was experienced as another world, stretching out towards the rocky rim of the unknown far-away. Friendship with the spirits of the wilderness could be useful, but was also risky. The feelings of the Iroquois towards these spirits was strikingly similar to those of Algonkian hunters towards the powers of the Underwater World.

Along the outer rim of the wilderness wandered the Stone Giant, Lord of the False Faces that inhabited the forests surrounding the world of human beings. Huge, hunchbacked and boastful, he had a twisted face, the result of a struggle with the Great Spirit in the beginning of time. In punishment for his pride, he was ordered to help human beings with his powers over disease. The common run of False Faces were occasionally met by hunters—frightening heads flitting among the trees. Always craving tobacco and begging for this product of the Indians' gardens, they offered in return their help against disease and their knowledge of herbs, products of the forest.

Dreams of False Faces during sickness made a patient eligible for treatment by and initiation into the False Face Society. This society was one of many religious organizations concerned with the preservation of health. Representing if not embodying the spirits, members performed private curing rituals and exorcised evil from the village in public ceremonies in spring and fall. In these perfor-
62 mances they wore a great variety of masks, each of them representing a False Face seen in dreams. Their disguise as crippled hunchbacks in ragged clothing referred to the miserable existence of the False Faces as outcasts in the wilderness.

There are many intriguing correlations in behaviour, symbolism and function between the Iroquois False Faces and the Wihtigokan among the western Ojibwa and Cree. These correlations, however, are but one aspect of a basic mythological structure shared by the Iroquoian tribes and their Algonkian neighbours.

Although it is certainly true that human culture does not consist of tangible objects alone, these frequently served to visualize man's interpretation of his environment. The essence of man is to be found in his ability to give meaning to his life and to everything around him. This spiritual aspect was present in even the most functional implements made by the Indians.

Improvisations on Some Ancient Melodies

The ethnographic study of Indian art traditions has been severely impeded by the assumption that "primitive" cultures were static by nature and that they existed in a timeless "ethnographic present". In the study of cultural history in other parts of the world, however, the recognition of art as a reflection of social and economic change has contributed greatly to our understanding of cultural developments. The problem touched upon here is a disciplinary one; whereas ethnologists focus on living societies for which historical information is usually not readily available, archaeologists and historians always confront the results of change over long periods of time.

Adding to the difficulty is the lack of sufficient documentation, a characteristic feature of most early collections of ethnographic artifacts. Any information as to precise origins was usually lost by the descendants of the collectors. Even where tribe and date were recorded, one still has to be cautious. Indians frequently preferred to sell pieces that they had acquired from other tribes, but white visitors were usually unaware of this practice.

Culture change was not something restricted to the period of European contact; what is often referred to as a "traditional" culture was but one phase in the life span of that culture. Usually the term refers to the cultural situation just before the impact of European influence changed the whole life-style of the people involved. Most of the artifacts in this exhibition might be called late traditional. That is, some European trade goods were already present, but their successful adaptation reveals that they had not had any disruptive effect on the native culture.

Up to now I have emphasized the characteristics common to the peoples represented in this exhibition. Although I do not wish to encourage the misconception that all Indians were alike, I should like to mention some of the shared aspects of native arts and crafts before elaborating on the regional differences.

Any discussion of Indian clothing fashions must take into account the Indian's own attitude towards clothing. Worn either on ceremonial and festive occasions or for protection against the weather, clothing was easily discarded at other times. Far from arousing any feelings of puritan shame, the human body offered a happy opportunity for adornment through painting, tattooing, and the attaching of various pendants to arms and legs, ears, nose and hair.

Fur robes were widely used as body wraps. Hunters and warriors wore the furred or feathered skins of animal and bird heads as caps. Leggings and moccasins were also in widespread use. The painted decoration of skin clothing revealed a marked sense of rhythm and colour. Very distinctive in the art of the North American Indians were decorative patterns composed of parallel straight lines, triangles and rectangles, combined into geometric compositions. Except for their smaller size, patterns of this type in the Northeastern Forest were identical to those on the Plains. Engravings on bone and stone surfaces were common everywhere as, of course, were decorations on pottery. Beyond these general features, however, we meet a vast range of forms and techniques that were distinctive to the individual regions.

63–64

The concept of culture area to explain regional differences is frequently used in popular works such as this catalogue. A culture area is largely determined by ecological factors, and as such it is a useful concept in the description of the economic and technological adaptation of man to a particular natural region. One of its major limitations becomes clear if we superimpose a map of linguistic regions upon the geographic demarcation of culture areas: the two do not correlate at all. Groups of closely related languages frequently inhabit parts of adjoining culture areas.

It will be obvious that such related tribes usually shared far more than just language; they also usually had similarities in social organization, religion and art. All else being equal, the geographical boundaries of a given art style would have to be found in the region where ecological factors were in balance with non-material aspects of the cultural heritage. Unfortunately, the reality is usually more complex at any point in time. Population movements, intertribal trade and intermarriage continually affected the nature and spread of regional and tribal art styles. Our present knowledge of Plains and Woodlands does not yet enable us to define and describe the large number of these art styles before 1850.

This unsatisfactory situation improves somewhat if we look beyond the frequently short-lived styles to the widespread and ancient traditions these styles were rooted in. It appears that two major groups of closely interrelated traditions met and intertwined in the regions represented in this exhibition. One of them had its prehistoric origin in the Ohio–Mississippi region and in areas even farther south, whereas the other centred in the northern forests of Canada and Siberia. During many centuries, both the Northern and Southern Traditions seem to have radiated ideas that were adapted to a large number of cultures. In order to avoid confusion with archaeological assemblages, I want to emphasize that the following summary of these traditions is restricted to their historical phase.

Whereas the Northern Traditions had their origin in a nomadic hunting complex, the Southern Traditions were based upon sedentary horticulture. Within the regions and time span under discussion, the Northern Traditions were carried by Algonkian-speaking peoples, while the Southern Traditions were carried by Iroquoian and Siouan speakers. However, centuries of contact between the two traditional complexes were reflected in the cultures of these three groups of tribes.

65–71   The arts and crafts of the Northern Traditions included long skin shirts of the parka type, leggings, a woman's dress supported by straps over the shoulders and with separate sleeves based on the legging principle, peaked hoods, moccasins consisting of a soft sole turned up over the foot and gathered to a separate piece over the instep, robes and other garments braided from strips of rabbit fur, the use of garters below the knee, pouches and knife sheaths worn on the breast by hanging them on a string around the neck, straps consisting of many separate strings, quill-wrapped and looped fringe, quillwork in its various techniques, moose hair used in false embroidery, painted and quillworked discs on the fronts and backs of shirts, and the decoration of birch bark by means of scraping. Some Plains tribes adapted this scraping technique but executed it on rawhide.

In the art styles of the Northern Traditions we are struck by the predominant use of bilaterally symmetrical patterns in asymmetrical compositions. The bilaterally symmetrical patterns probably had their origin in the popular feminine
72-75 pastime of biting patterns in folded sheets of birch bark. Opened and held up to the light, the dotted patterns were regarded as experiments and potential sources of new decorative patterns. Based upon the same principle, the split-animal style among the West Coast Indians may well have originated in the same Northern
77-79 Traditions. Asymmetrical composition is to be found on the opposite sides of woven pouches, pipe bags, shoulder bandoleers, moccasin side-flaps, and various other artifacts. These items were decorated with distinctly different patterns on either side or with the same patterns in different colour schemes.

Distinctly part of the Northern Traditions was the representation of the so-
80 called "lifeline", joint indications, and frequently the kidneys in the picturing of animal spirits or human figures. Having its origin in ancient Siberian cultures, this style is related to the worldwide X-ray style, which emphasized the vitally important internal parts of animal and human bodies. One might say that this feature reveals an intellectual approach to the subject, in contrast to the optical approach of our way of picturing animals. In North America, echoes of the Scytho–Siberian animal style are to be found in Eskimo engravings and the painted designs on Zuni Pueblo pottery, in the paintings on Blackfoot tipi covers and the engravings on rocks in Virginia, to mention but a few instances. Because of the great antiquity and wide diffusion of this art style, the original symbolism has long since been lost in the variety of reinterpretations. Nevertheless, it is evident that this art style has a magic quality and that it played a role in the practice of shamanism. In this connection, we should also mention the ritual use of red ochre as part of the Northern Traditions.

The Iroquoian population, native to the region around the eastern Great Lakes and the St. Lawrence Valley, functioned as a major way-station in the northward infiltration of Southern Traditions. Apparently having travelled along this route,
81-82 a curvilinear decorative art style reached the Indians in northern Quebec and the Maritimes, but ritualized warfare of a southern character did not expand beyond the Iroquoian tribes. Originating in the Ohio–Mississippi region, the Southern Traditions were carried by Siouan-speaking tribes into the northwestern Plains. The Algonkian tribes in the Great Lakes region appear to have acquired southern features from both Iroquoians and Siouans. Imported predominantly by the Siouan tribes, the mythological structure of Sky versus Underwater spirits acquired a central place in the spiritual life of the Great Lakes Algonkians, and faint echoes of its symbolism reached as far north as the Naskapi in Labrador.

Both Siouans and Iroquoians played an important role in the dissemination of a
83-86 highly developed naturalistic style of sculpture in stone and wood that reveals a particular interest in the human face, birds and animals, in that order. The artists produced bowls in the shape of human beings and animals, effigy pipes, masks, and statues of squatting human figures. These three-dimensional sculptures were frequently decorated with engraved patterns and inlaid with shell.

The influence of the Southern Traditions is seen in body tattooing, the removal of all hair from the head except for one or more ridges, and the elaborate use of feathers in, for example, headdresses and robes. The widely diffused arts and crafts stemming from these traditions included the roached headdress made of red-dyed deer hair, a poncho type of dress for men, the wraparound skirt for
88 women, moccasins consisting of a soft sole turned up over the foot and gathered in a seam running from toe to instep, twined textiles of vegetable fibres and buffalo wool, engraved shell gorgets, shell beads, tubular copper beads, colour-dyeing of deerskin and textiles, and the use of pipes and tobacco.

91-93 Reflecting the meeting of northern and southern influences, curvilinear patterns
of a bilaterally symmetrical character were distinctive to the art of the Iroquois,
Huron, Montagnais–Naskapi, Micmac, Malecite, and related groups in northern
New England. Mixture of the two major traditions is also shown in a range of
intermediate forms between the southern front-seam moccasin and the northern
type with separate instep or vamp. The front seam of the western Iroquois
94 moccasin was covered with a quillwork pattern suggesting a vamp, whereas the
eastern Iroquois and Huron used a moccasin with a long, narrow vamp, strongly
suggesting a compromise between the two major types. The Cree combine the
95 front seam with a short, wide vamp at the instep of the moccasin. The side-seam
moccasin of the central and northwestern Plains is either related to the southern
front-seam type or is an independent regional invention.

Possibly derived from the southern-style wraparound skirt, a full-length
woman's dress of distinctive type was adopted by the peoples of the Northeastern Forest and the northern Plains. This dress was sewn together down the
96 side, with the top part folded over. This folded-over top portion, hanging down
over breast and back, frequently was decorated with painted designs by the
Naskapi and the Swampy Cree or cut into long quill-wrapped fringes by the
western Cree. Blackfoot and neighbouring Plains tribes used the tails of two
deerskins to create the top fold of the dress. This was later given up, but the
idea survived among these tribes in the layout of decorative patterns on the
upper bodice of women's dresses.

Circular designs, painted on the front and back of men's shirts in the North-
97 eastern Forest, were executed in quillwork by the Indians on the northern and
98 central Plains. The Mandan and Hidatsa on the upper Missouri River developed
a distinctive type of quillwork, wrapped around a coil of buffalo hair. It has been
99 suggested that the Eastern Sioux adopted woven quillwork, but probably they
acquired such decorative strips from the Cree and Ojibwa towards the north.
From the late eighteenth century onwards, Northern Traditions on the Plains
were reinforced by the immigration of many population groups from the Northeastern Forest and the Great Lakes.

The recognition of the two traditional complexes discussed above may be of
help in identifying more-localized tribal art styles, which so far have resisted
classification. Our knowledge of early tribal art styles slowly increases in direct
ratio to the numbers of artifacts found and the time spent in studying them. It is
evident, for example, that within such widespread "tribes" as the Cree and
Ojibwa a number of regional art styles distinguished the various independent
bands. Although each local style was a dynamic phenomenon, it should be
possible to discern a sense of tradition underlying and interrelating the tempo-
rary fashions. At the moment, however, we cannot yet picture what Alexander
Henry saw when he reached a Cree Indian camp on the Winnipeg River in the
1760s, and noticed that "the dress and other exterior appearances of the Cristi-
naux are very distinguishable from those of the Chippeways and the Wood
Indians" (Henry 1969: 246).

The Lost Tribes Found Again

When Whites Were Welcome

Whatever attitudes we may entertain concerning colonialism, the phenomenon has produced classic examples of very different adaptations by native and immigrant to the same environment. However, in practically all cases, the exploitation of the land by colonists has drastically affected the traditional lifeways of the native population. Colonial enterprise may be considered successful to the degree that both parties benefit from the association. Obviously, this opinion is not shared by those who feel that traditional societies should be preserved in artificial isolation from the dramatic expansion of modern socio-economic relationships. Although the cultivation of collective guilt feelings is fashionable, it should be noted that in any colonial enterprise the common people never had any real choice of the role they were to play.

Canadian history had its roots in the fur trade (see Map 2), and specimens of Indian arts and crafts can tell us a great deal about our early history.

After several decades of annual visits by itinerant coastal traders, the first permanent European trading centres established in North America were the French settlements in the St. Lawrence Valley, founded early in the seventeenth century. Traders offered the Indians cloth, iron nails, knives, hatchets, beads, brass kettles and liquor in return for furs, preferably beaver skins. The native focus on hunting and the large number of furbearers in the region made this trade very profitable for both parties. In 1614, this example was followed by the Dutch in the Hudson River Valley. Both waterways afforded access to the vast and fur-rich region of the Great Lakes, and many colonial wars link the early rivalry between Montreal and Fort Orange—now Albany, New York—with the ultimate formation of Canada and the United States.

Succeeding the Dutch in the 1660s, the English intensified the competition by establishing trading posts on James Bay, the southern appendage of Hudson
101 Bay. By 1748, the Hudson's Bay Company imported glass beads, brass kettles, black lead, shot, brown sugar, Brazil tobacco, leaf and roll tobacco, thread,
103-109 vermillion powder, English brandy, wine, broadcloth, baize, blankets, duffels, flannel, gartering, lace, worsted binding, awl blades, buttons, burning glasses, bayonets, combs, egg boxes (!), gunflints, flintlocks, red feathers, fishhooks, fire steels, files, pistols, yarn gloves, goggles, handkerchiefs, laced hats, hatchets, hawk bells, ice chisels, knives, looking-glasses, crooked knives, needles, net lines, powder-horns, rings, barrels, sword blades, scrapers, scissors, spoons, shirts, shoes, stockings, worsted sashes, brass thimbles, tobacco boxes, leather trunks, twine, and cottons.

In the dawn of the new era for the aboriginal population, the traumatic spread of disease frequently loomed larger than the introduction of all kinds of new products. Unwittingly, the Europeans introduced measles, smallpox, typhus and many other diseases, to all of which the native population lacked immunity. Now here, then there, epidemics ravaged the regions reached by the fur trade and destroyed whole communities, while refugees carried the microbes even farther inland. Yet, native tribes continued to press for the establishment of trading posts in their territories throughout the history of the fur trade.

Far from waiting patiently for their customers to come to the trading posts,
adventurous traders penetrated deep into the interior, exploring and mapping
the country and stimulating the Indians to make the long dangerous journey to
the trading posts. Successful hunters were appointed as "chiefs" and rewarded
114 with red cloth and lace-decorated coats, plumed hats and silver gorgets. Alcohol
and tobacco were generously distributed as goodwill presents. In general,
however, these efforts met with limited success, giving rise to the emergence of
native middlemen who carried the trade far beyond the range of the European
traders. There is evidence that these middlemen utilized and expanded pre-
existing aboriginal trade networks. Shaming even the white traders, these native
middlemen made huge profits on the imported goods as long as they were able
to maintain their position. They tried everything imaginable to prevent the white
traders from breaching their monopolistic corridors, and rivalry over direct
access to the trading posts became a source of endless intertribal wars. If strong
enough, tribes in the interior defeated the former middlemen or drove them
away, then continued the lucrative business themselves.

Epidemics, the depletion of trapping grounds, and intertribal wars led to the
movement of populations over vast distances and to the emergence of new tribes
incorporating the remnants of many aboriginal socio-political units. This, in fact,
is the background of most surviving tribes, however much we tend to view them
as old traditional organizations.

The migration of Indians, away from the eastern scene of intertribal wars and
into the western Plains, acquired an extra stimulus when the spread of horses
made life more attractive in the "American Desert". Imported by Spanish
settlers in Texas and the Rio Grande Valley, horses became one of the highest-
priced items in the Indian trade. By 1740 the first horses had entered the
intertribal market in the Mandan villages on the upper Missouri River, where
they were met by the Assiniboine middlemen of the fur trade. Horses, guns, the
fur trade and the immigrant Woodland Indians provided the basis for the
dynamic development of the historic Plains Indian culture. It is significant that
we selected our romantic image of the North American Indian from this
hybrid culture; were the truly aboriginal cultures too strange to capture our
imagination?

For a correct appreciation of the widespread amalgamation of tribal traditions it
should be pointed out that not all migrations were westward. Fox Indians from
the Midwest settled among the Seneca Iroquois, who were forced to leave southeastern Ontario by the invading Mississauga in the 1730s; Ottawa and Nipissing
joined the Algonkin near Montreal; and Potawatomi descendants are still to be
found among the Eastern Ojibwa in Ontario.

By 1750, the approximate date the oldest specimens in the Speyer Collection
were produced, the fur trade had developed into a major and complex aspect of
colonial society, and its impact was felt by Indians as far to the west as the Black
foot. However, the centres of trade activity were still located on the rim of the
Northeastern Forest and in the region of the Great Lakes. Whereas only a thin
and tentative spearhead of the trade reached west of Lake Superior, the area east
of the upper reaches of the Ottawa River was already of decreasing importance.
French posts on Lake Ontario were maintained by means of government subsidy
in an effort to check the competition from the English.

The days when the Ottawa and Huron middlemen* made the long and dangerous voyage from the Great Lakes to Montreal and Quebec belonged to the past.
Now, large brigades of canoes, each carrying up to five tons of crew and freight,
were used to stock the French posts at Detroit, Mackinac, Green Bay, Nipigon,
and Grand Portage, as well as those on the upper Mississippi River. In
addition to these trading posts, the entire Great Lakes region was being infil-
trated by numerous independent traders, who lived with the Indians and
married into the tribes. Notwithstanding their small stock of trade goods, they
were of considerable importance in the dissemination of European technology,
such as the repair of firearms.

Since Europeans first arrived in the Indian country, the Métis had been steadily
increasing in numbers. They were accepted in neither of their ancestral societies,
and their wandering life was bound up with the westward-moving frontier of
the fur trade. The crucial role the Métis played as cultural brokers between
native and newcomer has long since been recognized.

The total value of the French-Canadian fur trade in 1761 was estimated at
£135,000, and would have been even higher but for the competing British, who
offered better quality at lower prices. English kettles and woollen cloth, in particular, were in great demand. The Cree preferred fine blue broadcloth, while the
Ojibwa and their neighbours insisted upon black and red cloth. Indians from as
far away as Lake Superior came to the British post of Oswego, and the more-
western Indians traded with the Hudson's Bay Company through Cree and
Assiniboine middlemen. As late as the War of 1812, however, the majority of
the furs from the Great Lakes and the Midwest reached Canada via Detroit,
Mackinac, and Grand Portage.

In the struggle between the French and the British, the Indians of the western
Great Lakes region were allied with the French, and the Iroquois with the
British. An intertribal federation fostered by Pontiac in the closing years of the
colonial wars failed because of the power already acquired by the Europeans and
the unwillingness of the Indians to return to a self-subsistent aboriginal
economy.

By 1750, the Ojibwa had emerged as a distinct tribal group through the merger
of a large number of independent bands along the northern shores of the Great
Lakes. The French-Canadian voyageurs and several tribes of Indians from the
St. Lawrence and Ottawa valleys contributed to the gene pool of the Ojibwa,
foreshadowing the later emergence of the Métis as a separate ethnic group. The
Ojibwa expanded their territory westwards when the focus of the fur trade gravitated first to Grand Portage on Lake Superior, and subsequently to the lower
Red River in present Manitoba. In permitting the Sioux to trade at the Great
Lakes posts, the Ojibwa had acquired access to their territory in return. With the
founding of French trading posts on the upper Mississippi, however, the Sioux
no longer tolerated the Ojibwa trappers, and protracted wars were the result. In
the course of these wars the Cheyenne were forced to leave their upper Red
River homeland, and the Sioux were pushed out of northern Minnesota and
Wisconsin. By 1800 the westernmost Teton Sioux had adopted a truly Plains
Indian way of life.

North of Lake Superior the Ojibwa penetrated the territory of Cree-speaking
bands, who were already slowly moving to the Saskatchewan country. The Cree
who stayed behind joined the newcomers, and this mixed population came to be
known as the Northern Ojibwa. As the Cree withdrew from southern Manitoba
the Ojibwa rapidly replaced them. Hardly identifiable yet as a distinct group, the
Métis explored the northeastern prairies, travelling in the company of their
Ojibwa and Cree relatives.

*The role of both Ottawa and Huron in intertribal trade had already started before the arrival of the
Europeans. According to one early French source, the term *Ottawa* means "trader" in the Huron
language.

By the end of the French regime in 1763, a chain of trading posts had been estab-
lished from Lake Superior past Lake Winnipeg and up the lower reaches of the
Saskatchewan. This placed the French traders squarely across the Indian trade
route to the British posts on Hudson Bay. After 1763, British traders from
Montreal and the Great Lakes inherited and expanded this western bridgehead.
As usual, the arrival of the trading posts was met with hostility by the Cree and
Assiniboine middlemen, who were losing their profitable position. An idea of
their profits is given by the price of a gun in 1760: the Hudson's Bay Company
demanded 10 beaver skins, the Montreal traders 20, but the Cree brokers 36
(Ray 1975: 180). Note also that, by that time, competition had already forced the
Cree to lower their prices. Finding that they now had to trap their own furs, the
Cree started to exert pressure on the Atsina and Blackfoot.

The competition from the "Montreal Pedlars" forced the Hudson's Bay
Company into more aggressive action. So far they had depended upon the
native middlemen to carry the furs down the Nelson River to York Factory.
Starting with Cumberland House on the Saskatchewan in 1772, Hudson's Bay
Company posts were established throughout the northern Plains, and contact
was made with the Mandan by 1804. The rivalry between the Hudson's Bay
Company and the Montreal Pedlars became yet more intense after 1783, when
a group of Montreal merchants founded the North West Company,
incorporating most of the Pedlars.

Problems of overseas transport and the necessity to reduce operating costs had
always forced Hudson's Bay Company personnel to live off the land, for which
they depended heavily on the James Bay Cree, their "Home-Guard" Indians.
The western expansion of the fur trade intensified the logistic problems of the
fur trading companies, and required them to maintain transportation routes that
grew ever longer. To cope with these difficulties, supply depots were constructed
at strategic points to provide the canoe brigades with food. As they lost their
former income from the fur trade, Indian communities along these routes shifted
from trapping to the gathering and trading of supplies for the depots. Corn was
bought from the Ottawa Indians at Mackinac, and wild rice from the Ojibwa at
Grand Portage. Referring to the western Cree and Assiniboine, Alexander Henry
reported that "the principal occupation of these people is making pounded meat
and grease, which they barter with us for liquor, tobacco, powder, balls, knives,
awls, brass rings, brass wire, blue beads, and other trinkets" (Innis 1956: 235).
The North West Company offered mostly lightweight imports and liquor in
return for food and small furs; and the distribution of alcohol reached frightful
proportions in the intense competition with the Hudson's Bay Company. At the
major posts of the Hudson's Bay Company, skilled workmen, such as smiths,
carpenters and tailors, were stationed to manufacture and repair trade wares for
the natives. Métis were hired as buffalo hunters, and more than 250 Ojibwa,
Ottawa, and Iroquois Indians drifted westwards as far as the Rocky Mountains
as peddlers and hunters for the traders. Owing to this development, cultural
distinctions emerged in this period between the Plains Cree and the Western
Woods Cree, and between the Plains Assiniboine and the Woods Assiniboine.
Whereas the Plains groups became food providers for the traders, the Indians in
the northern forests continued as fur providers.

In the cut-throat competition, the North West Company held the advantage as
long as its aggressive traders were able to make a quick killing in newly
penetrated regions. In the end, however, their long transportation routes were
their undoing. The staggering costs involved made competition more and more
impossible and monopoly control inevitable. When a new rival ascended the
Missouri River, the two Canadian companies merged in 1821.

One of the major effects of the merger was the cutting of the labour force by nearly two-thirds. Most of the men released were the Métis hunters, who settled on the edge of the forest and on the prairies in the lower Red River Valley. Rooted in two societies and two natural environments, the Métis emerged there as a distinct ethnic group in the 1820s. From about 500 persons in 1821, they increased to some 3,000 by 1850. In long trains of squeaking Red River carts the Métis set out on their annual buffalo-hunting expeditions, whose surplus meat they sold to the fur traders and the Selkirk colonists. The Métis started to manufacture large numbers of skin coats, moccasins and pouches, decorating them with colourful floral designs. Through trade and intermarriage, the Métis spread this art style among the northern Plains tribes. Their annual expeditions to St. Paul, Minnesota, included cartloads of this craftwork in addition to large numbers of buffalo robes.

189

Following the famous expedition of Lewis and Clark in 1805–06, American fur traders from St. Louis came up the Missouri River, which provided a relatively easy route into the northern Plains. Trade goods, which so far had been sparsely provided, were shipped up the river by the ton in large keelboats. The Mandan lost their profitable broker position in the trade, and Assiniboine and Blackfoot bands, pushing the Atsina aside, gravitated towards the new trading posts on the Missouri River.

Owing to the growing demand for leather by eastern industries and the easy transportation of heavy loads on the Missouri River, the export of buffalo hides became economically feasible. This development heralded the final, most dramatic chapter in the western fur trade. Indians, Métis and increasing numbers of white hunters brought about the destruction of the northern bison herds in the 1870s. The native world, grown rich and colourful with the imports of the fur traders, collapsed when they pulled out. By that time, the production of craftwork by the Indians of the eastern Great Lakes had long since been focused on the tourist market.

Innovative Indians

The most immediate and obvious effects of the westward-moving frontier of the New World have been sketched in the preceding section. Through the fur trade, the material culture of the Indians was enormously enriched; in addition to a variety of imported goods, many Indians acquired their first knowledge of European technology. So far, we have ignored the introduction of new ideas affecting the form and decoration of garments, containers and other utensils. However, the meaningful incorporation of these imports must be credited to native creativeness. This is true not only with respect to the material culture: throughout this period we perceive Indian manipulation of a wide range of concepts, aboriginal in origin but adapted to the changing environment. Significant, for example, was the emergence of behaviour patterns and techniques to incorporate the stranger, whether Indian or European, into ever-widening kin relationships. The Iroquois adopted Dutch, French and English colonial governors, at first as "Younger Brothers". They translated the European family names, turning them into titles. These titles were applied to their successors, reminiscent of the titles of the fifty hereditary Iroquois chiefs. The Indians made their first adjustments to Europeans in terms of existing native conditions. They were able to do so as long as, in a sense, they were protected by the fur trade. European settlement and the expansion of colonial power having taken place over a long period of time, the native societies in the interior were able to adapt gradually to increasing change. It is in this period that the Indians showed remarkable ingenuity and readiness to experiment with novelties.

Most simple was the direct replacement of native materials by imports without gross alteration of aboriginal forms and functions. The first steel hatchets replaced stone gorgets as prestigious adornments; metal cones attached to fringes replaced rattling devices made from the dewclaws of deer; copper kettles not only replaced pottery in daily use, but were frequently found in graves, placed upside-down over the heads of the deceased; copies of bone needles used for netting snowshoes were cut from sheet brass; brass and, subsequently, tin replaced the shell inlays forming the eyes of Iroquois masks.

124 Chipped as flint had been, bottle-glass made fine arrowheads, which also were available ready-made of iron at the trading posts. A larger-size steel point was **126-129** introduced that could be used as either the head of a spear, the blade of a knife or the point inserted into a war club, replacing stone prototypes. The effective use of steel knives is apparent in the skilful carving of wooden bowls, war clubs, and utensils made of wood, antler and pipestone. Some forgotten Blackfoot Indian took a metal can, punched holes all over the surface, and introduced this invention as a rasp to smooth the knots in tipi poles. The impact of metal on a stone-age world was memorized by the Osage Indians through a special religious ceremony.

130 The straightforward adaptation of imported materials is also illustrated in this exhibition by a beautiful sash. Braided strands of yarn were used to create a network by wrapping quills around them at regular intervals. This technique is clearly related to the former use of quill-wrapped and netted fringes by the Ojibwa, but is quite different from the netted sashes made by them in more recent years.

Manufactured fabrics gradually replaced fur and buckskin in the festive costumes of the natives. In the earliest days of the fur trade, the Indians restricted the use of full dress to their visits to trading posts; tattooing and body painting disappeared only with the adoption of everyday clothing. Woollen stockings were first used as tobacco pouches by the eastern Indians. Right from the start, however, blankets were popular, provided that the traders offered the right colours. Black, blue and red were preferred by the Indians, and white or light colours rejected. Old blankets were ravelled out, and the threads were used to replace hemp and buffalo hair in the weaving of bags. Pieces of red or blue stroud were boiled with porcupine quills to dye the quills a vivid hue.

With the exception of stroud and silk ribbons, the imported textiles did not lend themselves to the creation of cutout decorations, common in the skin clothing of the Indians in the northeast and Great Lakes regions. The trimming of stroud clothing by means of cut edges became popular among the northern Cree, who subsequently introduced it to the Athapaskan tribes on the Mackenzie River. Ribbon appliqué work appears to have started among the Huron and Iroquois, who in the early eighteenth century decorated their blanket robes with simple strips of silk sewn to the blanket. Large stocks of ribbons were dumped on the Indian market when the French Revolution enforced in France a rigid simplicity of dress. The subsequent abundance of silk ribbons in the fur trade enabled the **132-133** Indians to develop elaborate appliqué work, particularly in the Great Lakes region and the Midwest.

Imports were not restricted to those of European origin. With the expansion of intertribal contacts and their increased frequency, some culture elements once distinctive to small regions spread far and wide. The Iroquois probably acquired the blowgun in this way from the Southeast, and Iroquois trappers seem to have introduced the crossbow to some tribes in the Rocky Mountains. A type of **134-135** pipe bowl once restricted to the Indians of the Maritimes became popular as far west as among the Blackfoot. During the late eighteenth century the western Cree were rapidly adjusting to the Plains culture of their Assiniboine allies, as illustrated by their adoption of the Assiniboine warrior society and the Plains style of dress.

Aboriginal metalworking had been restricted to the cold-hammering of copper, which was found in almost pure form around Lake Superior, but even this was a lost art by the beginning of the seventeenth century. With the introduction of firearms, the Indians acquired lead and moulds to make musket-balls. It did not take them long to make their own moulds for casting buttons and pendants. Except for the pewter pipes made by the Seneca Iroquois in the seventeenth century, most casting was done in lead. Iroquois, Eastern Ojibwa and Potawatomi made pipe bowls of wood and antler, and lined them with lead.

Probably taking the idea from the handles of imported knives, the Iroquois used cast-in inlays to add extra weight to the heads of snow-snakes, the sliding
136-138 javelins thrown in a game. This technique became very popular for ornamenting and repairing stone pipe bowls. Channels were carved into the surface of the bowl, which was then tightly wrapped with leather and bark, and molten lead was poured into the carved channels. Apparently having started among Indians in Pennsylvania, the technique spread as far as the Sioux and Ojibwa around the western Great Lakes. In the course of this development, the Fox Indians discovered a lead mine near Dubuque, on the Mississippi, which they exploited as late as the 1820s.

As early as 1740, European traders offered silver ornaments in exchange for furs, and these superseded the earlier shell gorgets. Enormous quantities were produced especially for the Indian trade by silversmiths in England, Canada and
110-115 the United States. Between 1758 and 1762, about 8,300 silver ornaments were made for this purpose in Philadelphia, and comparable quantities were manufactured in Quebec and Montreal. In 1782 the trading post at Detroit alone needed about 18,600 silver items. With the decline of the fur trade the supply of these ornaments was cut off, stimulating the Indians to take up the craft themselves. In view of the westward-moving fur trade, it is not surprising to find the first native silversmiths among such eastern tribes as the Iroquois and Cherokee. By 1830, silverwork had been taken up by the Menomini and others south of the Great Lakes, but little if any of this work was ever done by Canadian Indians, except perhaps the Ottawa.

Braided and finger-woven sashes are still made by Indians in Wisconsin and Oklahoma, and the craft has been revived by the French Canadians. The complex historical relationship between the Indian and Quebec sashes has not yet been fully determined. However, it is significant that such fabrics were unknown in France, whereas the Great Lakes Indians had been braiding and twining sashes and bags since prehistoric times. Dutch sashmakers were active in the Hudson River Valley by 1650, when sash-like garters were fashionable in New England as well. French-Canadian activity does not seem to predate 1700, and we have no idea what these early sashes looked like. The consensus today is that finger-braiding originated among the Indians, and that it was adopted by the French Canadians in the mid eighteenth century. Improvements made
139 possible by the variety of textiles available to the French Canadians had reached the native societies by 1800. The fur trade played a major role in this process. Starting in the 1780s, large numbers of French-Canadian sashes were distributed by the traders as far away as Great Slave Lake. Significantly, the
140 Indians who started to make similar sashes all belonged to tribes that had been braiding sashes since precontact times.

The Indian's interest in novelties did not stop with materials and techniques; it is evident that he was intrigued by the forms of the white man's houses, garments and utensils. Hardly any aboriginal forms were left in the crafts of the Indians along the Atlantic coast by the time ethnologists started to record their culture. To a large extent this is true for the Iroquois as well. In place of their dome-shaped longhouses, they adopted the European ridged roof on vertical walls at an early date. Soon after the American Revolution, these bark dwellings were superseded by single-family log cabins. A two-runner type of sledge of French-Canadian origin is nowadays considered "traditional" among the Huron and Algonkin, who formerly used the toboggan.

Many of the new forms required the acquisition of European tools before they could be copied by the Indians. After the introduction of scissors, pouches made of whole animal-skins pretty well disappeared. Modelled upon military bullet-containers, square envelope-shaped pouches became popular throughout the eastern woodlands. At first these pouches, and knife sheaths as well, were worn over the chest on a neck-string. Later the European style of broad shoulder-straps was adopted. Ultimately this style survived only in the elaborate bandoleer pouches used by the Ojibwa on festive occasions. In the course of this development, traditional decorative patterns were cleverly adjusted to the form of these containers.

The terms the Indians used in referring to the first European explorers frequently reflect the curiosity of the natives with regard to some unusual feature of those whites. Thus the term "Coatmen" used by the Indians of New England implies that they were unacquainted with such garments. Except for one intriguing picture in Samuel de Champlain's *Voyages*, there is no evidence that coats were used by Canadian Indians before the eighteenth century. Indians in the Northeastern Forest wore long skin shirts or parkas, decorated with paintings around the hem and sleeves, and with quillwork on the shoulders.

After the arrival of white Coatmen in James Bay, the regional Cree changed their parkas into coats simply by cutting the fronts open. The price of this fashion was a loss in efficiency; Indians never added buttons to the opening, and a sash or belt had to hold the garment together. The earliest record of these skin coats among the Cree dates back to 1743, and the fashion appears to have spread rapidly throughout the Northeastern Forest region.

There is no need to assume that all Indian-made coats were derived from these long, straight northern coats. Those worn by the Huron in 1718 and those regarded as traditional among the Eastern Ojibwa by 1850 were certainly patterned upon cloth coats acquired from the fur traders. The tailoring of these 143 trade coats and of the redingotes worn by whites after 1750 was copied by the Labrador Naskapi after 1770 and by the Red River Métis around 1800. The Métis played a major role in the dissemination of these decorative skin coats throughout the northern and central Plains.

"Capotes", or blanket coats, replaced these skin coats after 1840, but the old style of decoration survived in a remarkable way. The striped Hudson's Bay blankets were cut in such a way that the coloured stripes formed a decoration around the lower part of the coat as well as around the sleeves, and the fabric was cut into fringes along the shoulders.

There is evidence that the Plains Indians, in adopting the horse from the Spanish Mexicans, also adopted their distinctive riding gear. However, a survey of Indian equipment clearly reveals that they were not slavish imitators. In their hands the
144 Mexican packsaddle changed into a sturdy cushion, allowing the native hunter
145 maximum freedom of movement. Lavishly decorated cruppers and martingales reflect the dashing colour of the Plains Indian culture in its heyday. Beautiful
146 gun cases originated from the same region; they were based upon a prototype that was imported ready-made by the Hudson's Bay Company in the 1770s.

The introduction of glass beads made an enormous impact on Indian decorative art, gradually replacing all other techniques, particularly where cloth fabrics superseded buckskin. Yet the Indians were acquainted with stone, bone, copper and shell beads long before the European replacements arrived on the scene. Thus, the study of the prehistoric use of beads appears to be more fruitful than attempts to trace the origin of the various historical beadwork techniques in the use of porcupine quills for decoration. The assumed relationship between woven quillwork and woven beadwork would be more convincing if the two techniques had been utilized in the same region. This is not so, however, nor is it true for netted quill-wrapped fringes versus netted beadwork. On the other hand, many decorative patterns found in early quillwork survived in the subsequent beadwork period.

The weaving of glass beads on a simple loom was preceded by the making of bandoleers with tubular copper beads during the fifteenth century by the central East Coast Indians. These copper beads were woven side by side, at a right angle to the warp strings, several rows of these beads constituting the width of the bandoleer.

Purple and white shell-beads, or "wampum", replaced these copper beads after the introduction of steel tools simplified their manufacture. The first wampum
147 belts appear to have been made in about 1620 by the Susquehannock in Pennsylvania, and some twenty years later they were reported among the Iroquois tribes. The use of wampum belts spread throughout the eastern woodlands after the Iroquois began to substitute them for sticks and skins in the confirmation of official messages (see page 19). The native preference for blue and white glass beads early in the fur trade clearly stemmed from the natural colours of the wampum beads.

148-151 Woven sashes, garters and bags were enriched by white bead decorations among the Iroquois and Great Lakes Indians. The beads were carried on a separate thread, and woven into the fabric in zigzag, diamond and hexagonal designs.

152 Bead embroidery may be related to linear quillwork in that both quills and beads were held in place by spot-stitching. However, a more convincing relationship is suggested by the shell-embroidered linear figures on the skin clothing of the central East Coast Indians. It may be significant that the earliest appearance of glass beads sewn into decorative patterns on clothing was among the neighbouring Iroquoian tribes in about 1640. During the subsequent westward spread of beadwork, various embroidery techniques were developed, such as the lazy
153 stitch and the Crow stitch, but space does not permit a more detailed treatment here.

In their contacts with the fur traders, the Indians were exposed to only a very small segment of European culture. If any non-material aspect of that culture ever crossed the language barrier during that period it had little meaning for the Indians, however superior some whites may have felt in that respect. Members of undamaged cultures usually feel too assured of their own beliefs to have any interest in exotic ideas. This situation certainly handicapped the Christian missionaries who penetrated regions as yet undisturbed by other agents of European civilization.

Long before they made any genuine converts, however, these missionaries made their presence felt through the instruction their schools offered in more practical subjects. Although acknowledging the influence of European folk art along the colonial frontiers, we find an excellent example of this mission activity in the development of the floral art style among the Canadian Indians.

During the French colonial period, several religious orders established mission schools in Quebec, Trois-Rivières and Montreal, where nuns trained Indian girls in everything considered useful for women in those days. Part of this education was fine embroidery, mainly in the floral designs of the French Renaissance. Probably as a result of visits to local trading posts with their parents, Indian girls were attracted from far and wide, although local Huron and "Praying" Iroquois
154-156 girls obviously predominated. Under the influence of the nuns, these Indians developed a distinct and very elaborate floral art style during the eighteenth century.

Many of the Huron and Iroquois moved west as trappers and canoemen in the service of the fur trade, whereas large numbers of Indians from the Great Lakes came annually to visit the French trading centres in the St. Lawrence Valley. Through these and various other means of contact, the floral art style gradually made its impact upon the native arts of the interior. Semi-floral designs incised on birch-bark containers reached the Mandan villages on the Missouri River by the late eighteenth century.

From the foregoing it will be clear that floral art among Canadian Indians began as a very elaborate and naturalistic style. On the basis of field research, however, Frances Densmore assumed that "in the development of Chippewa design an interpretation of nature through conventional flower and leaf forms preceded an imitation of nature" (1929: 186). More historical information and access to early collections enables us to correct this point of view. The "interpretation of
158 nature" Densmore speaks of resulted from the gradual adjustment of imported floral elements to aboriginal designs by tribes in the remote interior. Without direct and continuous contact with mission schools, these Indians were only occasionally exposed to the floral art of itinerant eastern Indians, and they could set their own pace in the selective adaptation of new ideas. It is noticeable that, with the westward expansion of Roman Catholic mission activities, an increas-
159 ingly floral art style superseded the semi-floral patterns that the western tribes had only recently developed.

Although there is evidence that the Indians transferred some of the symbolism of their traditional patterns to the new floral style, it is also clear that the ongoing change from magico-religious symbolism to more decorative art ran parallel with similar impoverishing developments in other aspects of their social life.

Indian Summer

Before winter comes to court us in his cold beauty, aging summer musters all that is left of her riches to make a proud but final stand. We call this period Indian summer.

By 1850, the end of the period covered in this exhibition, some of the Indian nations the eastern part of the country were already being split up into administrative units, called "bands", and scattered on reserves. Those farther west had achieved a satisfactory adjustment to life on the Plains as hunters, whose lives were closely allied with the skin and fur trade, and who were largely unaware of the collapse to come. Only the Métis had read the danger signals.

By that time, practically all groups now recognized as distinct tribes looked back on a period of continuous removals, enormous population declines, fusions with other groups, and the reintegration of heterogeneous cultural elements into new and relatively viable configurations. It had been a chaotic period in which tribal traditions had broken down and coalesced into regional Pan-Indian cultures, almost obliterating former local differences. Now that the smoke was clearing, the new or renewed tribes were emerging, as indicated by distinct tribal art styles. Although many of the old decorative techniques were still in use, new ones were gradually taking over.

Along with most of the economic activities of their rural white neighbours, the eastern tribes had adopted their dress for daily wear. The production of craft-work was largely confined to three types of activity: the mass production of such useful objects as snowshoes, canoes, splint baskets and moccasins, which were sold both locally and through wholesale outlets in eastern cities; the mass production of embroidered skin and bark trinkets for tourists at the growing number of summer resorts; and the manufacture of decorated garments and other paraphernalia for ceremonial use by the Indians themselves. Depending upon their location and degree of acculturation, some tribes produced mainly for the commercial market, whereas others did very little craftwork, and that largely for their own use. In the first group were the Huron, Abenaki, and Iroquois communities along the St. Lawrence River. The various Algonkin bands were typical of the more self-subsistent tribes.

Not surprisingly, the best craftwork in this region was to be found in the items made for Indian use. The style of the cloth ceremonial costumes revealed a complete amalgamation of native and early-European fashions. Repetitive series **160** of fine curvilinear designs, executed mainly in white beads on black, blue and red wood broadcloth, were distinctive to the Montagnais, the Maritime tribes, the Abenaki, Huron and Iroquois, and the Eastern Ojibwa bands as far as the Timagami. Ribbon appliqué, to the limited extent it was used, was combined with these beadwork patterns. Each of these communities developed its own distinctive features but, taken as a whole, the style was rooted in the old curvilinear tradition mentioned earlier (see p. 31).

161 Woven sashes were produced by the Iroquois exclusively for their own use, as were False-Face masks. Elaborately carved and painted floral designs decorated **162** the cradleboards of the St. Lawrence Iroquois at Saint-Régis, Caughnawaga and Oka. These designs look more like European folk art than anything else, and further research may well reveal the direct involvement of French-Canadian craftsmen. In less elaborate form this style was also found on cradleboards of the Oka Algonkin, who were in the process of moving up the Ottawa River and to Maniwaki, north of Canada's new capital.

Twined woven bags, wampum belts and other antique items, to the extent that they were still in use, acquired an almost sacred emotional value as heirlooms of the past, memories of which became increasingly distorted.

163-166 Floral designs executed in moose-hair embroidery on black-dyed skins were distinctive to the Huron at Lorette, near Quebec city. The decorations were used on their own festive garments as well as on various items made for the tourist trade. Completely commercial was their production of birch-bark trinkets embroidered with moose hair; this was a mission-taught craft that the Huron shared with the Ojibwa and Ottawa in the Great Lakes region. Also tourist-oriented was the manufacture of such items as moccasins, bags, caps and pincushions, decorated with a raised or embossed type of multicoloured beadwork in heavy floral designs. This work was distinctive to the Abenaki, the St. Lawrence Iroquois and the New York Tuscarora, and most of it was sold to the tourists visiting Niagara Falls.

167 Splint baskets, decorated with handpainted and potato-stamped patterns on the
    wooden strips, were turned out in huge quantities by the Abenaki, Huron,
    Iroquois, Ontario Delaware, and Mississauga. Wandering Indians sold these
168 baskets far and wide. Made by Algonkins and Montagnais, birch-bark contain-
    ers decorated with scraped floral designs were beginning to attract the more
169 adventurous tourists. The only surviving form of quillwork in the east was to be
    found on the birch-bark boxes made for the tourist market by the Maritime
    tribes, the Mississauga and the Ottawa.

Most of the old craft techniques were still alive among the Indians of the Great
Lakes region in the mid nineteenth century. These Indians still depended upon a
modified traditional economy of trapping, hunting, fishing, the cultivating of
corn, and the gathering of wild rice. Some of them found employment in the
slowly expanding lumber industry. Their everyday costume was a mixture of
European and native garments, but very elaborate costumes were worn on
ceremonial occasions. Stimulus for the manufacture of such decorated costumes
was largely derived from the ritual activities of the Midaywiwin, or Grand
Medicine Society, which had lodges in most of the native communities in this
region (see p. 28).

170 The characteristic ceremonial costume was made of black or blue cloth, velvet
171 being most popular. The use of black-dyed skins survived as a background for
    quillwork and beadwork on medicine bags. In the man's costume, trousers and
    aprons had replaced leggings and the breechclout, large bead- or silk-embroi-
    dered yokes and woven shoulder-strips decorated the shirts, and vests were as
    popular as turbans made of fur or of woven sashes. Highly decorative bandoleer
172 pouches, knee garters and numerous necklaces completed this costume. The
    woman's costume consisted of a wraparound skirt, a blouse covered with silver
    brooches, knee-length leggings, and a robe decorated with silk-ribbon appliqué
    work. Moccasins with a vamp over the instep were the most popular type, but
    the old toe-seam type of moccasin with enlarged and lavishly decorated ankle-
    flaps survived in some tribes south of the Great Lakes.

174-175 Characteristic of the Ojibwa was a flamboyant and realistic floral style of decora-
        tive pattern in bead embroidery. South of the Great Lakes, bead embroidery was
        executed in an earlier style of stiff and highly conventionalized semi-floral
        design units, mixed with diamonds, hearts, stars, circles, hands, and human and
        animal forms. More difficult to define are the tribal differences in woven
        beadwork, though this technique does not seem to have been very popular
    176 among the Ontario Ojibwa. Nor was ribbon appliqué, which was developed into
        very elaborate forms by the Potawatomi, Winnebago, and other tribes to the
        south.

177 Sashes and bags, sometimes interwoven with white beads, were made of yarn
    and various native fibres. Rushes, cattails, and cedar-bark fibres were woven into
    mats, whose geometric patterns were created by dyeing some of the fibres. Picto-
    graphs traced on birch bark with a sharp bone point served as memory aids
    during the rituals of the Midaywiwin. Painting was restricted to the heads of flat
    drums, which were decorated with dream figures of human and animal forms. A
    fair amount of woodcarving was done, mainly of wooden bowls and dolls for
    ritual use and fancy war clubs to be used for show in dances. The Ojibwa and
179 the Eastern Sioux excelled in the carving of spiral-shaped pipe stems and of
    stone pipe bowls inlaid with lead. Some silver ornaments were made by the
    Menomini, and conical metal jingles were being replaced by thimbles and
    woollen tassels. While attending each other's ceremonials, the Indians of the
    Great Lakes region enjoyed trading and giving one another their decorative
    paraphernalia; the frequently incorrect tribal attributions in museum collections
    reflect these activities.

Hardly started in this region, the tourist industry was restricted to hair-embroidered and quillworked birch-bark trinkets made by the Ojibwa, Ottawa and Menomini.

By 1850, Indian life in the Northeastern Forest centred on the stabilized fur trade. Trapping and fishing were the main economic pursuits, and most of the tools involved were of trade origin. Rituals in honour of the game spirits went on as before.

With the rapid decrease of large game after 1820, cloth had replaced moose and caribou skin in the dress of the Northern Ojibwa and Cree, a development noted among the Montagnais as early as 1808. Because of the scarcity of large skins, the Northern Ojibwa had adopted the Cree idea of braiding strips of rabbit fur into parkas and blankets. Only in the caribou-rich country of the remote Naskapi did the use of skin costumes survive. Whereas black and blue wool broadcloth were preferred by the Northern Ojibwa and Cree, red and blue were most popular among the Montagnais. Imported articles of European dress were considered prestigious because of their rarity.

A man's dress consisted of a breechclout, a parka, leggings decorated with oblong panels of beadwork down the sides, moccasins with a vamp over the instep and a central seam down to the toe, a long coat held together by a trade sash and with hood attached, a fur cap, and bead-embroidered garters with **180** woollen pompoms at the ends. The James Bay Cree sported cloth hoods lavishly decorated with beadwork, and often with a bunch of feathers or woollen tassels at the peak. Similar hoods were worn by the Cree and Ojibwa in Manitoba and by their Sioux neighbours to the south. U-shaped shot pouches hung on long straps over the shoulders of hunters.

The woman's costume consisted of a strap dress with detachable sleeves, a parka, knee-length leggings decorated along the bottom, moccasins of the same type as those worn by men, and a trade blanket used as a cape. Conical caps were popular among the Naskapi and Montagnais women. Both sexes wore their mittens attached together by a string hung around the neck.

In the decoration of clothing, aboriginal techniques survived mainly along the margins of this region; painted designs continued to embellish the skin costumes of the Naskapi, and woven quillwork that of the northwestern Cree. Among the intermediate Northern Ojibwa, Cree and Montagnais, bead and silk embroidery predominated. A limited amount of woven beadwork in small strips was made by the Naskapi, and silk ribbons were used along the edges of beaded surfaces by the Cree. Fringes on bags, garters and other items consisted of looped strings of beads and woollen tassels on strings of large beads.

Characteristic of the floral art style of this region were numerous small stylized flowers and buds distributed along a bilaterally symmetrical composition of stems; frequently they emerged from a vase design. Floral designs on shoulder straps and other long, narrow surfaces were usually arranged along an undulating centre line. The James Bay Cree embroidered rows of tiny leaves all along the flower stems, whereas the more-western Cree gave these stems a hairy appearance by means of many short diagonal lines emanating from them.

Introduced by the Cree, this floral art style exercised a strong influence on the art of the Mackenzie River Athapaskans in the nineteenth century. Of course, **181** the ancient geometric designs survived in the woven quillwork of the northwestern Cree and the woven beadwork of the Naskapi. The curvilinear painted designs of the latter represented the northernmost version of the old northeastern art tradition mentioned on page 43.

Artistic expression was not confined to clothing. Geometric designs were woven into the webbing of snowshoes, which were decorated with woollen tassels along the outer rim of the wooden frames. Crude designs were scraped on the surface of birch-bark containers; simple ones with religious connotations were painted on drumheads, bear skulls, snowshoes, canoe prows, the fronts of toboggans, and occasionally on the bark covers of wigwams. Some tattooing still 182 survived among the Cree and Montagnais. Pipe bowls were carved from grey soapstone and connected to short stems by strings of beads. Wood carving was largely restricted to cradleboards, spoons, ladles and dishes.

By 1850, Plains Indian culture was in its most glamorous phase, one that would have been impossible without the fur trade and the introduction of the horse; yet it was distinctly Indian in character. It was based on the buffalo and other game animals, which were the most important sources of food and raw materials. A tribe consisted of a number of nomadic bands, each of which was led by its own chief and had its own territory. Annual ceremonies, military societies and intertribal warfare were important factors in the achievement of tribal cohesion. Military prowess and wealth in horses served to determine social standing.

In contrast to the tribes on the western High Plains, however, those in the north eastern Parklands never put such emphasis on the acquisition of large herds of horses, whose relative scarcity among the Assiniboine and Cree resulted in the survival of buffalo pounds, the dog as a beast of burden, and small, lightweight tipis. Lack of horses also limited this people's involvement in the buffalo-skin trade. Whereas trapping of small furbearers continued to be profitable to the Parklands Indians, it never appealed to the Blackfoot, who preferred hunting buffalo on horseback and raiding neighbouring tribes to secure more horses.

The cultural differences between these two sub-regions were also reflected in their forms of artistic expression. The western style of material culture and decorative art was shared by the Blackfoot tribes, the Sarcee, the western bands of Plains Cree, and to some extent by the Assiniboine and the Atsina. The arts and crafts of these peoples were still predominantly traditional. Blanket coats and breechclouts were recent additions to their dress, which consisted of soft-soled side-seam moccasins, leggings, buffalo robes, long dresses for women, and ceremonial poncho-type shirts for men. Feathers were used in a variety of head ornaments, dance paraphernalia and shield decorations. In the Blackfoot woman's dress, the traditional folded tail of the deer skin at the top survived in the typical U-shaped pattern of beadworked bands over the breast and back. The characteristic Plains moccasin with separate rawhide sole had achieved limited popularity by 1870.

Buffalo robes were decorated with a long strip of quillwork or beadwork over the central seam, or were painted with horizontal stripes, columns of arrow designs, or realistic war records. The crude, stiff figures in these record paintings were archaic compared to the elaborate naturalistic style of painting developed by the Sioux on the central Plains. Pictographic paintings of war exploits and dream experiences were also executed on the large tipi covers, tipi linings, drumheads and shields. Geometric designs were painted on rawhide containers, and face painting was commonly practised by both sexes.

Quillwork remained a flourishing art as long as tanned skin was as readily available as red and blue stroud. The large size of the "pony" beads did not allow the execution of detailed patterns. This situation prevailed until about 1870, when small "seed" beads were imported in quantity. Virtually all the beadwork in this region was executed in the "overlay" stitch, done in straight lines.

Decorative quillwork and beadwork was of the geometric type: straight lines, rectangles, and triangular patterns constructed of many small solid squares. The designs were usually placed against a light-blue or white background, frequently surrounded by a frame of short diagonal lines. The design units and their bilaterally symmetrical composition betrayed ancient relationships with the Northeastern Forest tradition.

Although far less homogeneous, the arts and crafts of the Assiniboine, eastern Plains Cree, Plains Ojibwa and Métis formed a continuum of partially overlapping features, with the Assiniboine and the Métis at the two extremes. The woodland origin of the Parkland style was clearly recognizable, but in its adjustment to the prairie environment there was a pronounced influence from the central Plains through the Assiniboine.

Although the basic costume of the Parkland Indians was similar to that of their western neighbours, red and blue stroud already had largely replaced animal skins, and blanket robes and coats were far more common than buffalo robes. Women wore the eastern strap-dress with detachable sleeves, and their moccasins were of the vamp type. The cloth hoods of the men were similar to those of the Cree in the Northeastern Forest. Tattooing was peculiar to the Cree, although face painting and extensive use of feathers was common among all Plains Indians.

185

The Red River Métis sported caps and top hats encircled with silk ribbons, trade sashes wrapped around blue stroud coats, and knee-length leggings worn over the trousers. A decorated knife-sheath and tobacco pouch were usually attached to the man's sash. Derived from an early Ojibwa prototype, these oblong cloth pouches were decorated with a panel of woven beadwork attached to the bottom and surrounded by woollen tassels on long strings of beads. The designs executed in woven beadwork were very distinctive and of a complex geometric type. Another pouch type developed among the Métis was the so-called "octopus" pouch, decorated with four long tabs at the bottom. Both pouch types were introduced by the Métis to the northern Athapaskan tribes; in museum collections they go under all sorts of tribal names, but their Métis origin is rarely recognized. The same is true for most other craftwork of the Red River Métis. Yet, these people made large quantities of highly decorated skin coats, pouches, moccasins and horse gear, which they traded all over the northern and central Plains.

186

187

Quillwork was on its way out by 1850, to be replaced by beadwork and silk embroidery. Woven beadwork and a little ribbon-appliqué work was produced by the Plains Ojibwa and Métis. The geometric designs, woven with quills and subsequently with beads, were clearly related to those of the Cree and Northern Ojibwa. In their complexity, however, they foreshadowed the geometric style that became distinctive to the western Sioux in the 1880s.

188

Most characteristic of this region was the floral style of decoration. It had many features in common with the semi-floral designs popular around Lake Superior, but in the hands of the Métis women the style acquired a quality rivalled only by that of the Huron in the East. Frequently emerging from hearts or discs, the bilaterally symmetrical plant designs consisted of fine, curving stems and sparsely distributed delicate leaves. Three such leaves together usually took the place of flowers at the extremities of the stems. Another characteristic feature was the large number of different colours used in a single composition without being garish. The impression of the style is that of a sparkling delicacy.

189

This floral style started between 1800 and 1820 among the Red River Métis,
marking their emergence as a distinct ethnic group. The Sioux called them the
190 "Flower Beadwork People". Their floral art rapidly became popular among thei
Ojibwa and Cree relatives. Trading their colourful craftwork far and wide, the
Métis introduced the new style to the Assiniboine and Eastern Sioux, who dev
oped distinct tribal varieties after 1830. Subsequently adopted by the latter's
191 western relatives, the Sioux style favoured imaginative compositions of geometric and floral units combined into long, climbing patterns. After 1870, Siou
decorative art again became predominantly geometric, but the new patterns
were still identified as "leaves", "the fork of a tree", and similar floral descriptions. By that time also, the Blackfoot had adopted the floral art style. It is
significant, however, that the western Plains tribes restricted the use of floral
designs mainly to the types of items that the Métis traders specialized in:
moccasins, coats, pouches and horse gear.

In the development of Métis art a gradual shift is noticeable from Ojibwa to
Cree influence. This change appears to reflect the removal of the Métis to
Saskatchewan in 1870, after their nationalistic aspirations were suppressed by
the Canadian Government. Fifteen years later these aspirations were finally
crushed in the second Northwest rebellion. As seen through the part of our
history that is sketched in these pages, the Métis emerge as the culmination of
truly Canadian cultural development. The promise held out by this fusion of
two cultural traditions failed to materialize, and the defeated Métis turned out
be the disturbing herald of our long struggle for a Canadian identity.

Catalogue of Artifacts

Note Where the tribal name is qualified by "type", a tribal attribution has been arrived at through research, rather than on the basis of documentation received with the artifact.

48

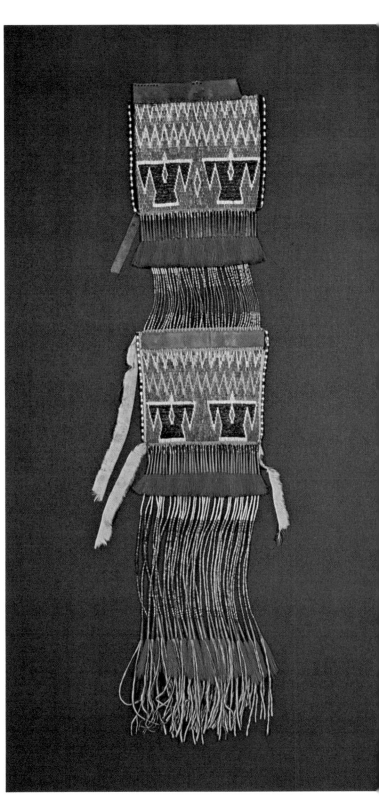

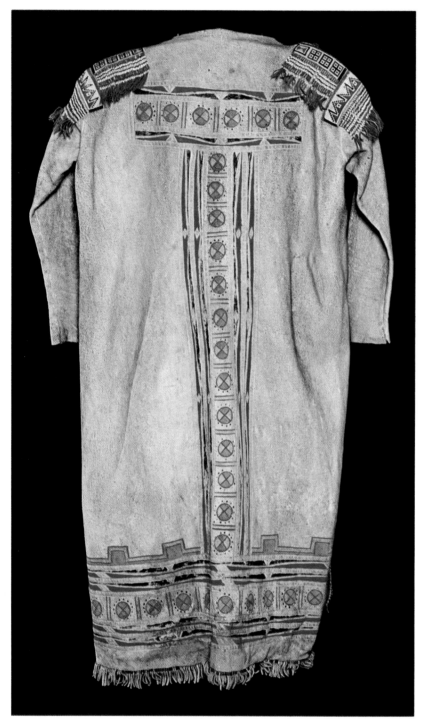

63

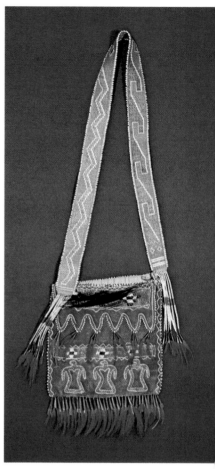

78

126

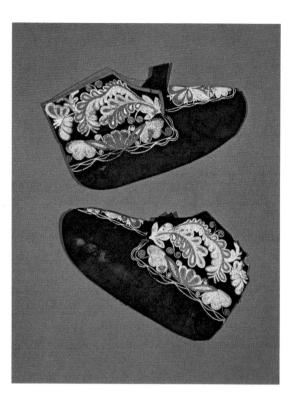

155

158

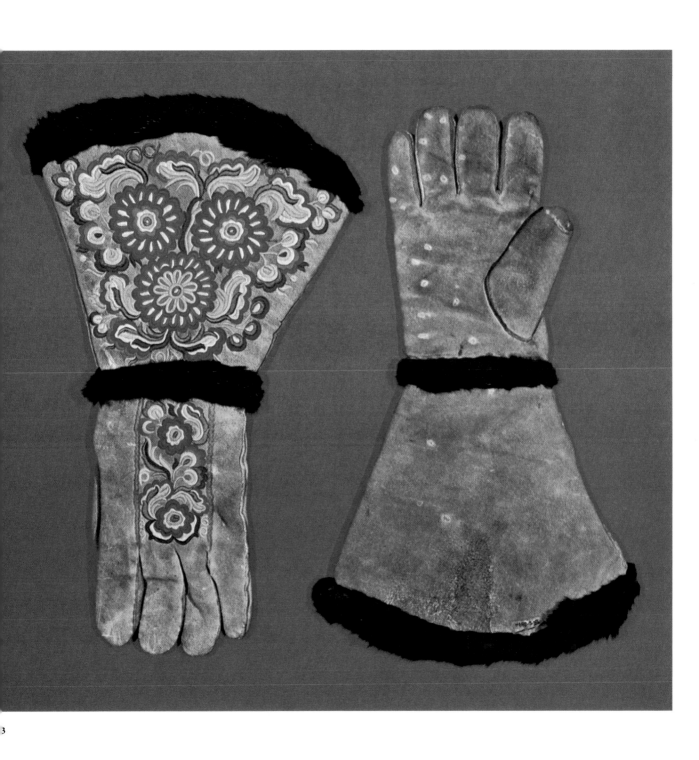

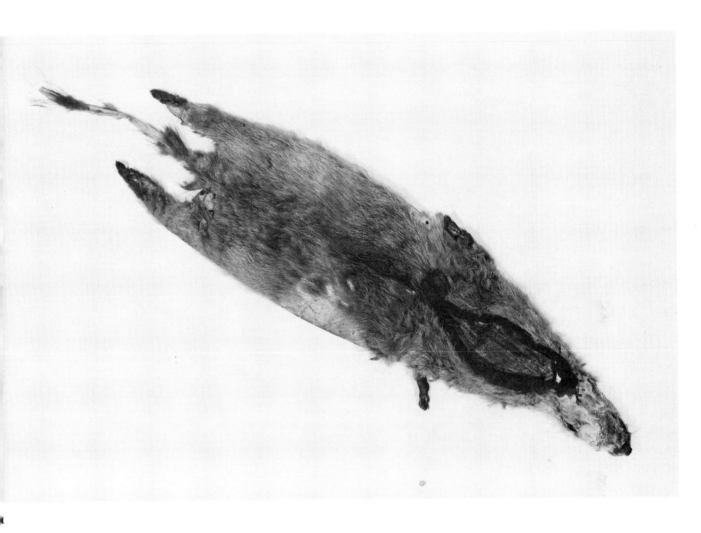

Pouch
Tinder pouch made from complete weasel skin.
Vertical slit on underside, edges bound with
brown cotton.
L. 46 cm
Eastern Canada, before 1825

Speyer Collection; previously in the collection of
Harding, a German Privy Councillor, who acquired it
in July 1825.
NMM III–X–231

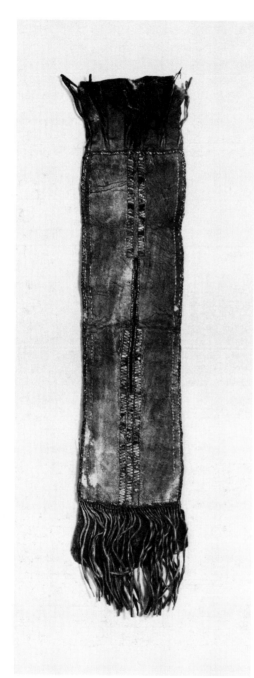

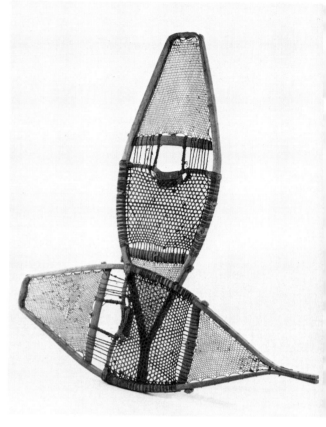

3

Snowshoes
One-piece frame of hardwood with two wooden
crossbars. Hexagonal-weave mesh of rawhide
thong in foot space, and of commercial string at
either end; at heel end, mesh is repaired with
vegetable-fibre twine. Frame is wrapped at
middle with canvas and rawhide. Iron rivets
secure ends of frame at tail, and tufts of wool
are attached to outside edge of frame. Inner
edge of frame has been carved into double curve
at toe.
L. 110 cm
Ojibwa type, nineteenth century

Speyer Collection
NMM III-G-821

2

Pouch
Shot pouch made from tanned, smoked skin
decorated with red and black porcupine-quill
appliqué. Centre slit down one side. Edges of slit
and sides of pouch are bound with quills; lanes
of quills extending from slit are attached in
zigzag-band technique (worked over two
threads). Cut-skin fringes are attached at both
ends, backed with an extension of the pouch at
bottom. Sewing and quillwork are with sinew.
L. w/o fringe 45.5 cm
Iroquois, before 1800

Speyer Collection; previously in the collection of the
Duke of Hessen-Darmstadt.
NMM III-I-1314

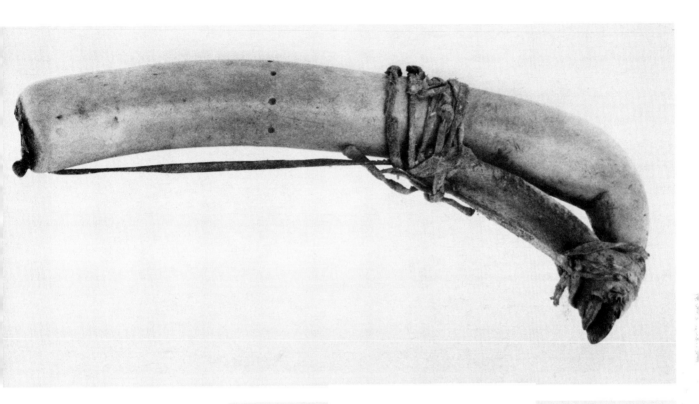

Skin-Scraper
Antler-elbow type, with iron blade encased in tanned skin and anchored at top and part way down handle with thongs. Extension of thong is drawn through hole in handle end. Row of small holes is incised around handle, and four metal tacks are inserted in handle end.
L. 32 cm
Blackfoot, c. 1860

Speyer Collection
NMM V–B–416

5

Container
Oblong container made from single rectangular piece of elm bark. Both ends are bent into an upright position, folded accordion style, and bound with strips of inner-bark fibre.
L. 30 cm
Iroquois (Seneca), 1912

Collected by F. W. Waugh from Alex Snider on the Tonawanda Reservation, New York, in September 1912
NMM III–I–754

6

Bag
Flat bag of twined basswood-bark fibre. Design
of three vertical stripes formed by introducing
bark dyed brown and black into the warp.
H. 19 cm
Ojibwa, before 1912

Collected by F. W. Waugh from J. Beaver on the
Chippewas of the Thames Reserve, Ontario, in 1912
NMM III-G-73

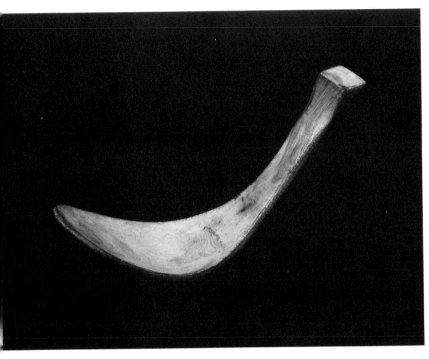

7

Spoon
Carved from spruce wood.
L. 24.5 cm
Cree, 1960s

Collected at Fort George, Quebec, in September 1967.
Made by Clifford Lameboy of Fort George.
NMM III–D–293

8

Club
Ball-headed type, of wood, with laterally
flattened head. Handle rounded toward end,
becoming flat-sided toward head. Handle end
carved into animal (bear?) head with eyes of
inlaid white glass beads. Skin thong drawn
through hole near end of handle.
L. 50 cm
Iroquois type, eighteenth century

Speyer Collection; formerly in the James Hooper
Collection, England.
NMM III–I–1312

9

Pipe Bowl
Made from black pipestone (steatite).
Ornamental crest with openwork design. Incised
rings around bowl opening and two sides of
stem-base opening; edges of crest have also been
marked with parallel grooves.
L. 12 cm
Ojibwa, c. 1850

Speyer Collection
NMM III-G-825

10

Ladle
Deep trough-like ladle made from mountain-sheep horn. Short handle, apparently broken off at top.
L. 25 cm
Blackfoot, c. 1860

Speyer Collection
NMM V–B–421

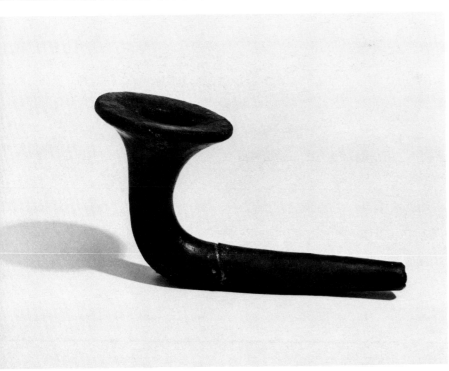

11

Pipe
Pottery, trumpet-shaped, brown in colour.
L. 14 cm
Huron, 1500–50

Collected by C. A. Hirschfelder in southern Orillia
Township, Simcoe County, Ontario, in 1884
NMM VIII-F-8408

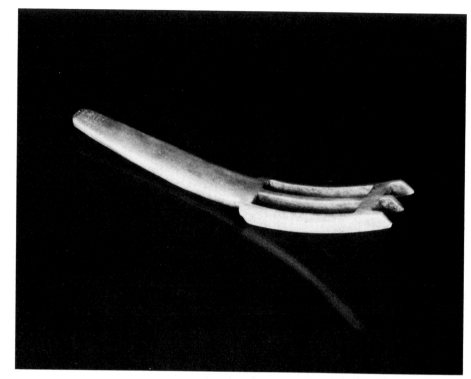

12

Paint Stick
Three-tined paint stick carved from caribou
antler. Used for painting parallel lines on skin
clothing.
L. 16.5 cm
Naskapi, before 1930

Collected by Duncan C. Burgess at Fort Chimo,
Quebec, c. 1930
NMM III–B–124

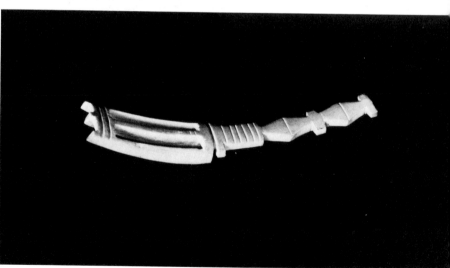

13

Paint Stick
Three-tined paint stick of caribou antler, with
carved handle.
L. 14.5 cm
Naskapi, before 1930

Collected by R. White, Jr., at Nain, Labrador, c. 1930
NMM III–B–231

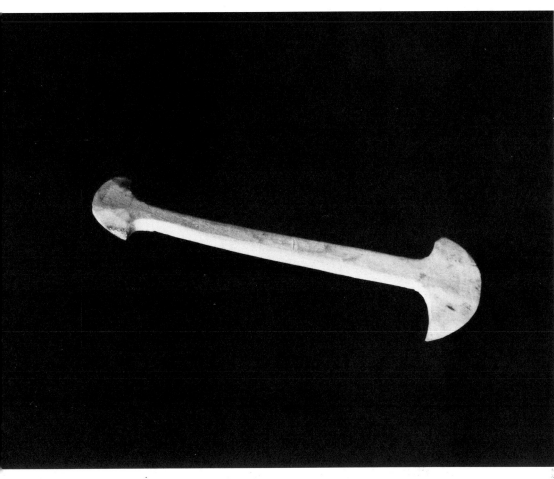

14

Paint Stick
Double-ended paint stick carved from caribou antler. Used to make curved designs on skin clothing.
L. 11 cm
Naskapi, before 1930

Collected by R. White, Jr., at Nain, Labrador, c. 1930
NMM III-B-234

15

Paint Bones
Five pieces of porous bone, used to paint red, yellow, green, blue and black patterns on skins.
L. 7.2 cm
Sarsi, 1921

Collected by D. Jenness on the Sarsi Reserve, Alberta, in 1921
NMM V-D-36

16

Paint Materials (not illustrated)
Yellow and red ochre, and charcoal.

17

Leggings
Made from soft unsmoked, tanned caribou skin.
Each is in one piece, seamed down outer leg,
with broad seam allowance to the outside.
Edges of seam allowances are cut into short fringes,
and were probably originally quill-wrapped.
Painted designs are in red, green, and deep
yellow achieved with fish glue, which yellows
with age. Sewn with sinew.
L. 77 cm
Naskapi, before 1770

Speyer Collection; formerly in the collection of the
Grand Duke of Baden.
NMM III-B-591

8

Boy's Robe
Boy's robe made from entire skin of buffalo calf.
Painted on hairless side with simple line draw-
ings of arrows in dark brown. Rents in skin are
seamed with sinew.
L. 2.15 m
Piegan, before 1833

*Acquired from the Museum für Völkerkunde, Berlin.
Formerly in the collection of Prince Maximilian zu
Wied. (Maximilian of Wied, 1782–1867, German
prince and naturalist, came to America in 1832
accompanied by the Swiss artist Carl Bodmer. They
left St. Louis in April 1833, visited trading posts on
the upper Missouri, and spent the winter of 1833–34
at Fort Clarke, in Mandan territory. They returned to
Europe in July 1834.)*
NMM V–B–280

19

Pouch
Made from tanned skin dyed dark brown, with
porcupine-quill appliqué. Fringe of thongs with
spiral wrapping of thin brass strips terminates in
tassels of red-dyed hair. Quillwork consists of
the outline of a bird on each side, in simple line
stitch, a wavy line in the same technique edging
the bag, transverse bands in zigzag-band
technique (worked over two threads), and quill-
piped seams. Quill colours are black, blue, red,
orange and natural white. Sewing and quillwork
are with sinew.
L. 46 cm
Ojibwa, before 1780

*Speyer Collection; formerly in the Greatorex Collection,
Whitechapel Museum, London, and later in the James
Hooper Collection, England.*
NMM III–G–822

20

Moccasins
Made from tanned, smoked skin. Each moccasin
is fashioned from a single piece, seamed vertically at the heel and up the front. Seams are
covered with porcupine-quill appliqué in zigzag
band and simple line techniques. Downturned
ankle flaps are similarly decorated, and edges
are bound with quills. Tassels of metal cones,
thongs and red-dyed hair are attached along
lower edge of ankle flaps and either side of
front seam. Quill colours are orange-red, faded
blue and natural white. Sewing and quillwork
are with sinew.
L. 25.5 cm
Eastern Great Lakes, late eighteenth century

Speyer Collection
NMM III–X–232

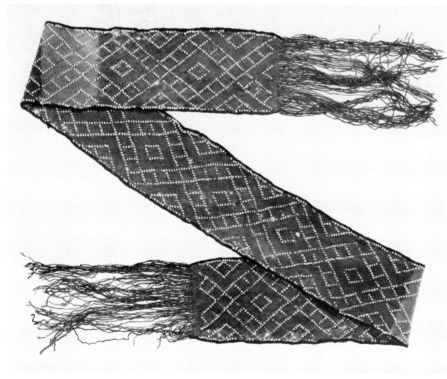

21

Sash
Finger-woven, using threads made by twisting
together ravellings from commercial wool cloth.
Natural dyes have been used: deep ochre-red,
with two transverse bands in yellow (produced
by either resist or discharge technique). White
pony beads of irregular size strung on blue
cotton have been worked in with the yarn,
producing a diamond-shaped pattern. Edges are
trimmed with black wool. A blue cotton thread
is twined through each end of the sash. Fringes
are of twisted double strands.
L. w/o fringe 132 cm
Eastern Great Lakes, c. 1780

*Speyer Collection; formerly in the collection of Sir John
Caldwell, fifth baronet, Castle Caldwell, County
Fermanagh, Ireland. (Caldwell served during the
American Revolution, from 1774 to 1780, as an officer
of the Eighth Regiment of Foot. He was stationed
briefly at Niagara, and then sent to Fort Detroit. His
official duties included frequent trips to Indian villages
in the surrounding area, and participation in several
councils with Indian tribes of the Great Lakes region.
He was elected chief of the Ojibwa Indians, who gave
him the name "Apatto", or Runner. [Source: Arthur
Oswald, "Sniterton Hall, Derbyshire. The Home of
Mr. and Mrs. Bagshawe",* Country Life, *2 Feb.
1961, pp. 228-31.])*
NMM III–X–230

Container
Made from birch bark, with thong carrying
handle. Seams are stitched with split and peeled
spruce root; rim is reinforced with wooden
splints and bound with roots. On the exterior,
most of the dark inner bark has been scraped
away to form designs of moose, hunter, woman
and dog.
. 38.5 cm
Timagami Ojibwa, 1913

Collected by F. G. Speck at Lake Temagami, Ontario,
in 1913
NMM III-G-254

23

Moccasins
Made from tanned, smoked skin. One-piece
construction. Decorated with porcupine quills
applied in zigzag-band and simple line
techniques. Downturned ankle flaps edged with
blue silk ribbon and white seed beads. Sewn
with cotton thread and sinew. Quill colours are
turquoise, green, orange and white.
L. 22 cm
Iroquois (Seneca), before 1830

Speyer Collection; formerly in the Fred North
Collection, London.
NMM III–I–1310

24

Moccasins
Pair of unfinished moccasins. Each is made from a single piece of heavy tanned skin, sewn down the outer curved side with sinew, and left uncut and unsewn at the heel. Decoration consists of a large rosette of coiled quill-and-hair-wrapped hanks of white horsehair sewn to tanned-skin base. Open centre is of red stroud. Quill colours are cream, brown, and orange; hair is dark brown. Beneath each rosette is a trapezoid-shaped area of woven quillwork, worked directly on the skin. Colours are cream and orange, plus brown from maidenhair-fern stems. Rosette and woven quillwork are outlined with opaque deep-turquoise glass beads. Sewing and beading are with sinew.
Moccasins made for intertribal trade by upper Missouri River tribes were left unsewn at the heel; the purchaser finished them to his own size.
L. 32 cm
Mandan–Hidatsa type, early nineteenth century

Speyer Collection; previously acquired in England by an Amsterdam dealer.
NMM V–H–3

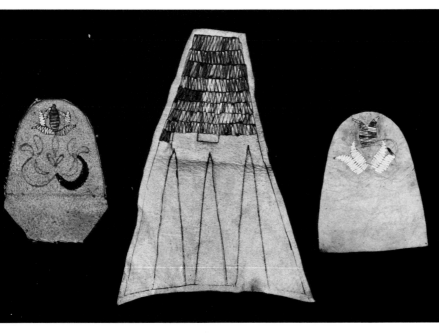

25

Moccasin Vamps
Three moccasin vamps. The one on the right is of fine tanned, unsmoked skin, with a stylized floral design that was first drawn in yellow pencil, then worked in pale-blue and purple porcupine quills. Sinew is used to secure quills. At left is a tanned, smoked skin backed with heavy canvas, with a layer of brown paper between canvas and skin. There is a partially worked stylized floral design in purple, green and maroon quills. Designs are drawn on the skin in pencil. The centre vamp is of tanned, unsmoked skin, with designs drawn in black ink. The narrow end is solidly quilled in purple with a partially completed cross design in green. Quillwork is with cotton thread.
L. of longest through centre 18.5 cm
Eastern Sioux, 1956

Collected by Mrs. Angus McKay at Griswold, Manitoba, in 1956
NMM V–E–206a, c, d

26

Pouch
Front made from sealskin, back from blue
stroud. Inside divider of red stroud. Across fro
are stitched two broad bands of loom-woven
quillwork, with a double row of translucent
green glass beads at either end. Quill colours a
red, yellow, green and natural white. Skin
fringes at base of quillwork are quill-wrapped,
with red wool tassels at ends. Pouch seam has
piping of fringed white skin, each strand strun
with white, rose and green, or white and purp
glass beads, with quill-wrapping and red wool
tassel at end. Trim at top is of gold and red gla
beads. Sewing, beading and quillwork are with
sinew.
L. w/o fringe 24 cm
Swampy Cree, before 1840

Speyer Collection; acquired from a "Miss Halifax a
Hudson's Bay".
NMM III-D-565

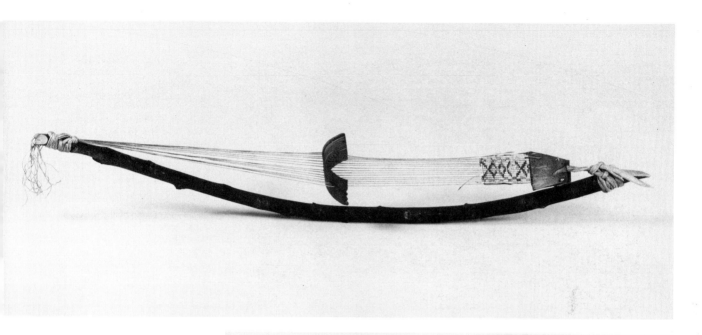

rcupine-Quill Weaving on Frame

w loom with cotton-twine warp stretched
ough two pieces of birch bark and fastened to
rved stick at each end. A piece of porcupine-
ill weaving has been started; colours are red
d purple against a natural white background.
52 cm
hltan, 1915

lected by J. A. Teit at Cassiar, British Columbia,
1915
AM VI-H-21

28

Sash

Made from fine thongs wrapped together in
pairs with porcupine quills. Free-hanging fringe
at both ends is formed from paired quill-
wrapped thongs, bunches of red-dyed hair, and
metal cones. Designs worked down length of
sash are in black, yellow and natural white
against a background of orange-red.
L. w/o fringe 120 cm
Eastern Great Lakes, eighteenth century

Speyer Collection; formerly in the Lamarepiquet Collec-
tion, Staatliches Museum für Völkerkunde, Munich.
(Lamarepiquet was a French biologist.)
NMM III-X-233

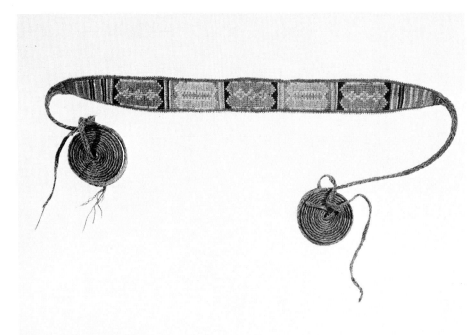

29

Burden Strap
Made from Indian hemp; twined weave in
middle section, with warp strands braided
together to form tying strips at both ends.
Middle section is edged with opaque white por
beads, and decorated with moose-hair false
embroidery, the colours being white, blue,
orange and dark brown. This technique involv
wrapping moose hairs around weft threads
during the weaving.
L. 5.0 m; centre section 60 cm
Iroquois type, before 1770

*Speyer Collection; formerly part of the Greatorex Col
tion, Whitechapel Museum, London.*
NMM III–I–1330

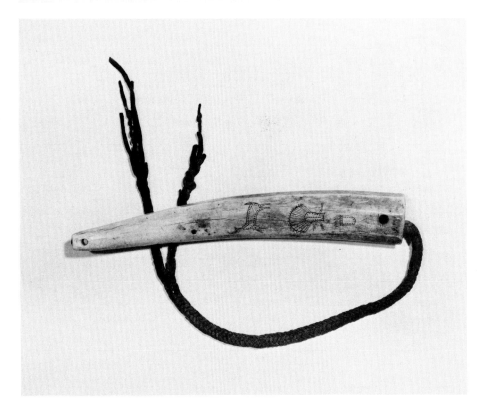

30

Whip
Made from elk horn, polished and slightly
faceted. Lash is secured by looping it over a
wooden peg that is inserted in the butt end of
the handle. Lash is eight-strand braided thong,
separated into two braids at end. Handle is
incised with blackened lines and dots; on one
side are two bear claws, on the other a deer,
bear claw, and fan with "arms".
L. handle 30 cm
Eastern Plains Siouan type, 1800

*Speyer Collection; formerly in the James Hooper Colle
tion, England.*
NMM V–X–394

dress

h headdress, made from deer hair (dyed
nd yellow) and porcupine hair (natural)
ted around commercial-thread base. Bone
n-spreader is inserted inside the long fringes
e headdress and secured with thongs. There
hree plume-holders (two bone cylinders,
f rolled skin) with eagle feathers. Green
 on one feather and cylinder.

5 cm

ha, before 1850

Collection

M V–Q–2

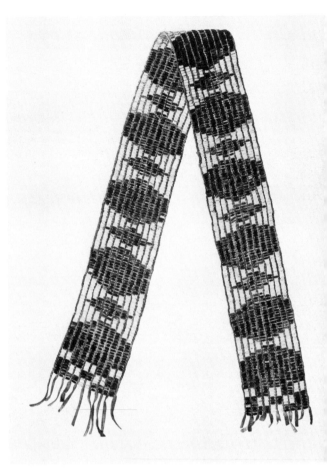

33

Wampum Belt
Eleven warp strands of thongs interwoven with
shell *(Venus mercenaria)* beads strung on
commercial thread. Design of large truncated
diamonds alternating with small complete
diamonds, in purple against a background of
white beads.
L. 98 cm
Eastern Great Lakes, eighteenth century

*Speyer Collection; formerly in the collection of the Earl
of Warwick, Warwick Castle.*
NMM III–X–234

32

Pouch
Made from tanned skin, with red-painted
designs on both sides consisting of a serrated
band down either side and transverse rows of
circle and ladder designs. A thong drawstring is
laced around the top edge. At bottom is a broad
panel of thongs and porcupine quills in netted
technique; colours are red, gold, black and
natural white. Fringes are of quill-wrapped
thongs, metal cones, and red-dyed moose hair.
Sewn with sinew.
L. w/o fringe 44 cm
Eastern Ojibwa type, c. 1780

*Speyer Collection; formerly in the collection of Sir John
Caldwell (see No. 21).*
NMM III–G–824

34

Prescription Stick
Smooth-surfaced wooden stick, engraved on
both sides with picture writing. Red and traces
of green and black painting.
L. 42 cm
Prairie Potawatomi, c. 1800

Speyer Collection; acquired from a dealer in Munich.
Formerly part of the Floyd Schulz Collection of Kansas
Potawatomi material.
NMM III–Q–1

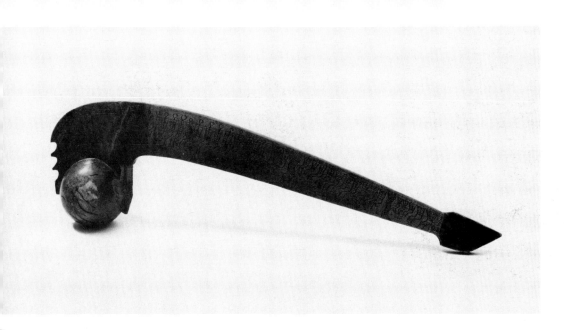

5

lub
all-headed type carved from single piece of
ood, with head formed from natural knot. Flat-
ded handle with slanted butt. Butt end and
pper and lower surfaces of handle have been
urn-marked; other surfaces have been stained
d. Thirty-one stylized human figures are
cised on one side of the handle, possibly repre-
nting a war party.
. 57.5 cm
reat Lakes, eighteenth century

eyer Collection; formerly in the collection of the
niversity of Göttingen, West Germany.
MM III–X–236

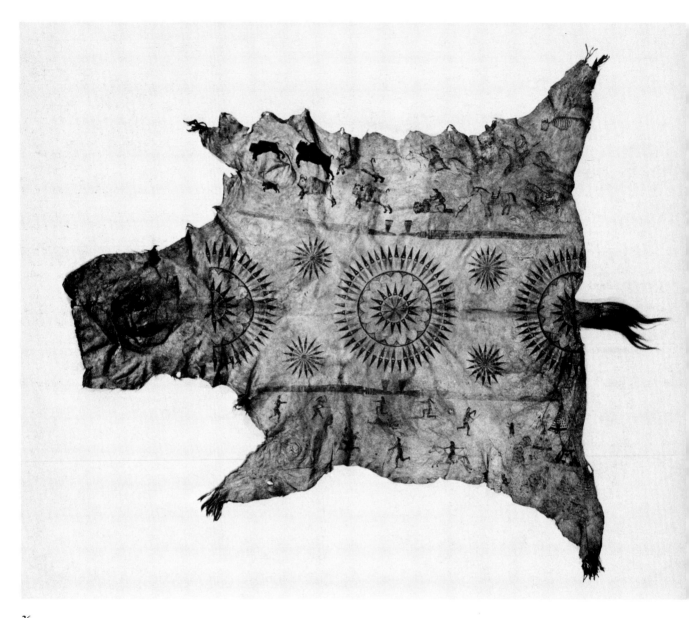

36

Painted Robe
Horse skin with greyish white hair, hairless side
painted in red, black, brown, yellow and green.
Design area divided into three parts by four
calumets painted lengthwise: middle section
shows sunburst motifs; upper part, buffalo-
hunting scene; lower part, camp scene with tipis
and war episodes. Cotton thread used to repair
tears in skin.
L. through middle: 2.3 m
Sioux type, 1843

Speyer Collection; collected by Gabriel André on the
upper Missouri River in 1843.
NMM V-E-281

37

Man's Shirt
Poncho type, made from two tanned skins. Skin
strips decorated with porcupine quillwork in
band technique are attached over shoulders and
down sleeves. Along one edge of each strip are
attached "scalp locks"—bunches of black,
brown, grey, or red (dyed) human and horse
hair, each bunch quill-wrapped and strung with
a blue glass bead at base. Triangular skin
pendants at neck, front and back have quill-
wrapped fringes and decorations of blue and
white pony beads. A small blue and white bead-
wrapped skin bundle is attached at one side of
neck opening.
On front and back, warriors are drawn in dark-
brown outline; some are shown with weapons
pointing to various parts of their bodies, presumably illustrating how they were killed. On each
sleeve twelve heads are drawn along the edge of
the quilled strip, and hoofs and dots are painted
on the sleeve extensions.
Sewing and quillwork are with sinew; small
amount of commercial thread used for repairs.
Quill colours are white, yellow, orange and dark
brown.
L. 120 cm
Mandan, before 1832

Speyer Collection; acquired from a dealer in Hamburg,
West Germany.
NMM V-H-2

38

Headdress
Circular cap of tanned skin on metal frame,
lined with yellowish cotton and red wool cloth.
Cap is surmounted by a pair of deer antlers and
edged with upright eagle feathers. There is a
long train of fringed tanned skin with a median
row of feathers, some bound with red wool
cloth at base. Cap ties are wrapped with sinew-
strung white and blue glass beads. Pendant
thongs around face are strung with tubular bone
beads and large trade beads. Forehead fringe of
cowrie shells strung on fine thongs. Beaded
forehead band of seed beads (white, with
designs in blue, yellow and red) attached by lazy
stitch to tanned-skin base. Trailer is painted
yellow except for fringes, which are painted red.
H. w. horns 40 cm; L. train 175 cm
Eastern Sioux, 1820s

Speyer Collection; acquired from the Berkeley Galleries,
London, c. 1952–53. Previously acquired by Captain
J. C. Phillips, of Gateshead, England, at Wounded
Knee, South Dakota, in 1892, with the information
that it originally belonged to Chief Little Crow
(1803–1863), Chief of the Kaposia-Mdewakanton
Sioux, who added the trailer and feathers after his
father's death in 1828. In the battle of the Little
Bighorn in 1876, this headdress was said to have been
worn by Chief Rain-in-the-Face (1835–1905), a Teton.
The beadworked brow band apparently dates from that
period.
NMM V–E–257

39

Pipe Bowl
Effigy form carved from black stone, with
tubular bowl representing human head facing
the smoker. Seated on the base is a figure carved
in relief in front of the bowl. At the stem end
are the remnants of a projection, which has
broken off.
L. 11.5 cm
Ojibwa type, c. 1845

*Speyer Collection; formerly in the collection of Sir
Daniel Wilson, Toronto.*
NMM III–G–823

40

Breast-Piece
Made from raccoon skin, the legs, tail and head
backed with red stroud. Red, green, beige,
yellow and ivory silk-ribbon appliqués and ties.
Quill-wrapped rawhide slats, and thong fringes
wrapped at intervals with quills. Tassels of dyed
horsehair, quill-wrapped thongs, and large glass
beads. Ornate metal-button eyes. Sewn with
sinew and cotton thread. Lengthwise slit in pelt
so that it can be drawn over the head.
L. w/o fringe 99 cm
Eastern Sioux, 1860

*Speyer Collection; formerly in the collection of the
Museum für Völkerkunde, Vienna, which acquired it
from Ward's Science Supply, Rochester, N.Y., in
1879, labelled Dakota.*
NMM V–E–282

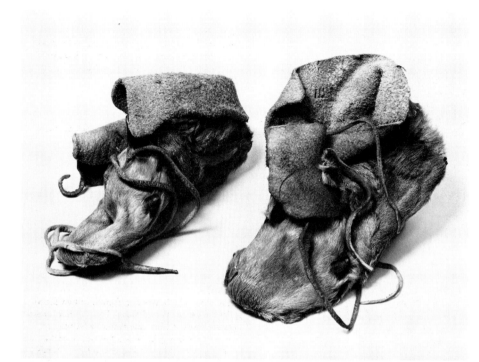

41

Moccasins
Made from leg skins of deer, with hair, hoofs
and dewclaws retained. Ankle flaps are of heavy
tanned and smoked skin. Thong ties. Sewn with
commercial thread.
L. 27 cm
Iroquois, before 1911

Collected by Chief John A. Gibson in Tuscarora
Township, Six Nations Reserve, Ontario, in 1911
NMM III-I-193

42

Shield
Of heavy buffalo rawhide, painted in two shades
of green, in charcoal grey and white, and
decorated with eagle and smaller feathers. Quill
ends are attached with sinew wrapping to
thongs. Some of the feathers are stained yellow
and green.
Shield cover is of tanned, unsmoked deerskin,
with lacing tie around the outer edge.
Diam. 54 cm
Crow, before 1842

Speyer Collection
NMM V-L-28

43

Moccasins
Unfinished; made from tanned, smoked caribou skin. At front, skin is gathered around set-in vamp, which is sewn with sinew. Painted designs in blue and red.
L. 32 cm
Naskapi, before 1914

Collected by E. W. Hawkes at Davis Inlet, Labrador, in 1914
NMM III-B-17

44

Snowshoes
"Beaver-tail" style wooden frame, in two pieces spliced together at mid sides. Toe and heel crossbars are mortised into the frame. Webbing of fine rawhide thong in hexagonal weave, with geometric designs incorporated. Strand of red-dyed thong is carried around outside of frame at toe and heel. Commercial-thread tassels in pink, green, dark red and white are attached to frame at toe and heel.
L. 60 cm
Montagnais, before 1924

Collected by F. W. Waugh from Eli Fontaine, a Montagnais, at Seven Islands, Quebec, in 1924
NMM III-C-484

45

Moccasins
Made from tanned white (unsmoked) caribou
skin. Basically one-piece construction, with
addition of downturned ankle flaps. Seamed
vertically at heel, and gathered and seamed
down centre front. Entire exterior, including
sole, is painted in deep yellow (derived from
fish glue, which has yellowed with age), red and
blue. Sewn with sinew.
L. 26.5 cm
Naskapi, before 1780

Speyer Collection; formerly in the collection of the
Grand Duke of Baden.
NMM III-B-592

46

Moccasins
Made from tanned, smoked skin. Soles are
decorated with transverse lines of red
porcupine-quill appliqué in zigzag-band
technique. Same technique used on vamp quillwork, where the design is worked in pink and
faded mauve against a red background. Two
lanes of lazy-stitch beading around sides as far
as heel; bead colours are blue, red and green,
plus a few faceted brass beads, against a white
bead background. Sewn with cotton thread.
L. 20.5 cm
Sioux type, early twentieth century

Acquired in 1953
NMM V-E-296

47

Rock Medicine
In the centre is a small ammonite (fossil shell)
covered with tanned skin. Decoration of transverse and pendant thongs strung with beads of
stone, shell (including wampum, dentalia,
cowrie and abalone), porcelain, metal, and glass
(including old Spanish blue glass beads). Also
attached are an animal tooth, twisted ermine
skins, a piece of scalp with hair, and an ear.
Suspension cord of twisted thong.
Ammonite 6 × 6 cm
Crow, c. 1860

Speyer Collection
NMM V-L-26

48

Painted Skin (colour plate, p. 51)
A rectangle of tanned, unsmoked caribou skin,
edges fringed and originally wrapped with red
porcupine quills. Designs on face were painted
in red and turquoise, and with fish glue, which
has turned deep yellow with age. The short tab-
extension at each corner is cut into a six-strand
fringe, each strand quill-wrapped and strung
with a brass cone and (originally) a tassel of red
hair. The red-painted border around the skin
was originally decorated with diagonal lanes of
red quillwork in zigzag-band technique.
105 × 118 cm
Naskapi, c. 1740

Speyer Collection; formerly in the collection of the
Grand Duke of Baden.
NMM III-B-588

49

Pouch
Made from tanned caribou skin, with four
fringed trapezoidal tabs at bottom. Designs in
red, black, and yellow from the fish glue that
has yellowed with age are painted on both sides.
Sewn with sinew.
L. 41 cm
Naskapi, before 1780

Speyer Collection; formerly in the collection of the
Grand Duke of Baden.
NMM III-B-594

50

Pipe Bowl (Cast)
Made from bluish-black stone, with salaman-
der-like carving. May have had a wooden stem
attached originally.
H. 8 cm
Iroquoian, c. 1600

Collected by T. Brasser in 1974
Private collection

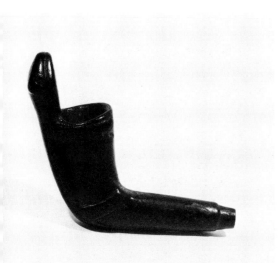

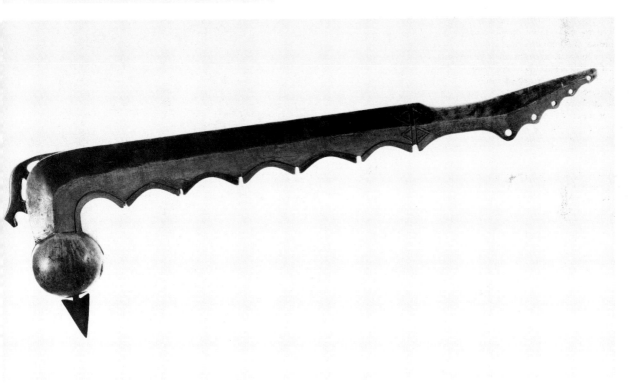

ɪb
ɪl-headed type, of wood, with central ridge
wn either side of the handle and the slanted
tt. Underside of handle is carved into deep
llops and that of the butt in shallower ones.
ı animal (panther?) is carved near the head.
e triangular iron point is a later addition. A
le in the head has been filled with lead. The
ıb is painted half red, half black, and there are
ised lines on the handle.
65.5 cm
eat Lakes, before 1840

eyer Collection
ʌM III–X–235

52

Painted Skin
A tanned deerskin, the inner wrapping of a war
bundle. Painted in black, red and yellow.
L. 110 cm
Menomini type, nineteenth century

Acquired from a dealer in Paris in 1965
Lit.: Skinner 1913: 103–17
NMM III–N–34

3

Rattle
Made from deer hoofs and dewclaws, each threaded on a thong and attached to the wooden handle. Upper end of handle is carved into a thunderbird head, and the other end is tapered to a point so that the rattle can be set upright in the ground at the end of a ceremony.
L. 19.1 cm
Ojibwa, before 1929

Collected by Diamond Jenness on Parry Island, Lake Huron, in 1929
NMM III-G-395

54

Cradleboard Decoration (colour plate, p. 52)
Two panels of quill-wrapped thongs interwoven in netted technique, with a pair of thunderbirds worked on each panel. A strip of tin is attached at the top of each panel. Between panels, the thongs are quill-wrapped, and a free-hanging fringe in the same technique extends from the bottom. There is a compact row of tin-cone and hair tassels at the bottom of each panel, and similar tassels are attached to fringe ends. Quill colours are orange, turquoise, black, white and small amounts of yellow.
L. w. fringe 86 cm
Ojibwa type, eighteenth century

Speyer Collection; formerly in a French collection, and marked "Georgian Bay" on an old label.
NMM III-G-848

55

Calumet
Fire-blackened wooden stem decorated with
porcupine-quill wrapping, wild-duck skin, and
strands of red wool. Five eagle feathers threaded
together in a fan shape with thong are attached
to underside. Each feather is secured to a quill-
wrapped wooden splint, with tufts of down
feathers also attached. Quill colours are black,
white, blue, yellow and red, plus orange on
stem. Both sinew and commercial thread have
been used in quill wrapping.
Bowl of greyish stone in flared form, with raised
grooved section around base.
L. 90 cm
Ojibwa, before 1830

*Speyer Collection; formerly in the collection of the Duke
von Coburg-Gotha.*
NMM III-G-826

56

Drum
Frame is a nailed hoop of wood, over one side
of which deerskin is tightly stretched. A thong is
laced around outer edge of cover, and thong
cords across back hold skin secure. A raven's
wing is attached with rawhide thong to underside of drum.
Red ochre is extensively used, particularly on
the wooden frame, thongs and wing feather. On
the drumhead, painting is in red, black and
green, with a double transverse line in black and
green. This style of painting indicates an association with a medicine-pipe bundle.
Diam. 40 cm
Blackfoot, before 1929

*Collected by H. I. Smith at Gleichen, Alberta,
in 1929*
NMM V-B-185

57

Pipe
Bowl of red pipestone (catlinite) with lead inlay.
Stem is of light wood, carved to give twisted
effect. Incised designs at both ends of stem are
painted red and blue.
L. bowl 14 cm; L. stem 63 cm
Eastern Sioux, early nineteenth century

Acquired from a dealer in New York in 1974
NMM V-E-292

58

Headdress
Cylindrical form of birch bark covered with
blue blanket-cloth. Appliqués of red and green
wool tape, wool and cotton cloth, silk ribbon,
and white glass beads. Four woodpecker heads
are attached at front, with yellow and blue silk
ribbons threaded through beaks. Hawk, eagle
and eagle-down feathers and several animal tails
are attached around top of headdress; the eagle
feathers are secured to quill-wrapped wooden
splints (quill colours are white, orange, blue and
black).
H. w/o feathers 20 cm
Ojibwa, before 1845

Speyer Collection
NMM III-G-827

59

Pouch
Made from black-dyed tanned skin, with porcu
pine quillwork in zigzag-band and simple line
techniques; a large thunderbird flanked by two
smaller ones is depicted on pocket face. Edging
of alternating white and deep-purple glass
beads. Tassels of thongs, brass cones and red-
dyed hair are attached in pairs on upper pocke
and were presumably originally attached along
bottom edge as well.
Quill colours are orange, white and black. Sine
has been used for quillwork, and sinew and
cotton thread for sewing. A carrying strap was
originally attached.
L. 27 cm
Ottawa, late eighteenth century

Speyer Collection; formerly in the collection of the Duk
of Gotha.
NMM III–M–2

60

Pouch (colour plate, p. 53)
Made from black-dyed tanned skin, decorated
with porcupine quillwork in three techniques:
one-quill edging, simple line, and zigzag band.
Figures worked on pocket face are horned
underwater panthers. Quill colours are orange,
red, yellow, blue and white. Sewing and quillwork are with sinew.
18 cm square
Ottawa, before 1800

*Speyer Collection; formerly in the James Hooper Collec-
tion, England.*
NMM III-M-1

61

Medicine Bag
Made from complete otter skin, with vertical
slits on underside of neck. Head cavity stuffed
with skin pouch. Underside of opened-out tail is
decorated with porcupine quillwork in zigzag-
band and simple line techniques, and brass bells
and purple silk ribbons are attached at tail end.
The four limbs are wrapped with a cord of
porcupine quills worked over two sinew threads.
Pendant brass thimbles strung on thongs are
attached to each leg, as are quill-wrapped
thongs, which are strung at ends with a copper
or tin cone and a bunch of red-dyed hair. Quill
colours are white and red. Sewn with sinew.
L. 113 cm
Iowa, c. 1850

Collected by M. R. Harrington in Oklahoma in 1910
NMM V-N-4

62

False Face Mask
Carved from a single piece of wood, with two
lengths of black horse tail, with skin, nailed to
rim. Crooked mouth, broken nose, deep
wrinkles are those of the first False Face. Metal
plates for eyes, and bindings of cotton cloth.
Painted black, indicating that the tree from
which the mask was carved was selected in the
afternoon. Inner edge of mouth and nostrils
painted red. Two small bundles, one of cloth
and one of paper, attached at top; these undoubtedly contain sacred tobacco.
H. 31 cm
Iroquois, c. 1850

Speyer Collection
Lit.: Ritzenthaler 1969
MMM III-I-1317

63

Man's Coat (colour plate, p. 54)
Long, straight, collarless style with centre-front
opening. Made from heavy tanned, unsmoked
moose hide, the body from a single piece, with
the sleeves added. Epaulettes of woven porcupine quills at shoulders; each band has blue
glass beads at ends, and a tacked-down fringe of
quill-wrapped thongs along sides. Fringe ends
are of ochre-dyed thongs and red hair-tassels.
Quill colours are red, yellow, black, white and
ochre. Front opening and bottom edge of coat
are cut into short fringes and quill-wrapped.
Designs are painted in bands across upper back,
around lower edge, down either side of front
opening, and down centre back. Colours are red,
yellow, blue and black. Unpainted impressed
borders were probably originally filled in with
fish glue. Sewn with sinew.
L. 135 cm
Northern Ontario, c. 1780

Speyer Collection; formerly in the collection of Sir John
Caldwell (see No. 21).
NMM III-X-229

64

Burden Strap
Woven belt of Indian hemp, with warp strands braided together at either end to form tying straps. Central portion is in twined weave, with edging of opaque white pony beads, and false embroidery on front in white, yellow, orange and blue moose hair.
L. 5.92 m; centre section 61 cm
Eastern Great Lakes, c. 1780

Speyer Collection; formerly in the collection of Sir John Caldwell (see No. 21).
NMM III-X-237

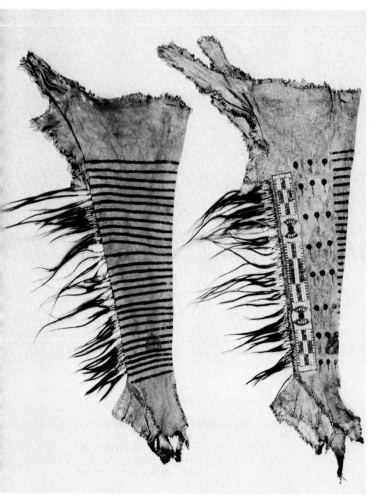

65

Leggings
Made from tanned, unsmoked skin, with painted designs and porcupine quillwork. Fronts are painted with tadpole designs and blotches of orange paint, backs with transverse bands in dark brown. A strip of heavy tanned skin covered with porcupine quills in band technique (including two rosettes) is attached down outer leg. Quill colours are white, red and turquoise. Fringe of locks of predominantly brown human hair and red, green and white horsehair attached down outer edge of quilled band. Each lock is wrapped near base with sinew and porcupine quills. There are trailers and an inset gusset at bottom of leggings. Unseamed edges cut into fringe. Sewn with sinew.
L. through centre front 109 cm
Blackfoot, 1840

Speyer Collection; acquired from Commodore Walzer, Salisbury, England.
NMM V-B-415

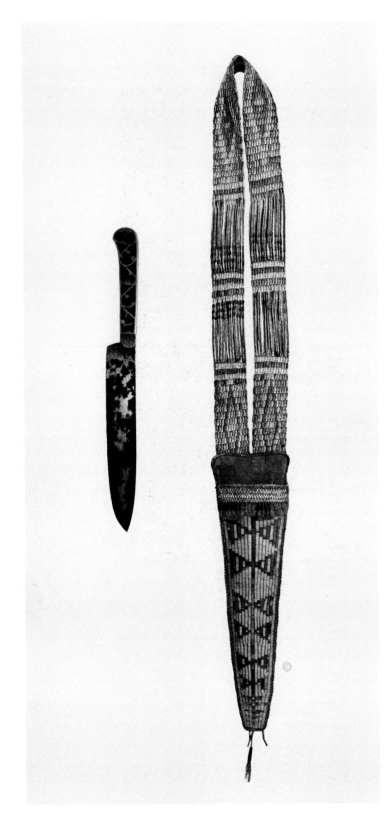

66

Knife
Iron blade marked "A. Hatfield". Handle of
brass inlaid with black material, probably
tortoise shell.
L. 24.5 cm
Eastern Great Lakes, before 1800

Speyer Collection; formerly in the Schwarz Collection,
Museum für Völkerkunde, Vienna. (Johann Georg
Schwarz went to North America in 1820–21 as a fur
trader. He was American consul in Vienna in
1827–48, where he was connected with the Austrian
missionary society Leopoldinenstiftung, through which
he added to his North American collection.)
NMM III–X–238

Knife Sheath
Made from two pieces of tanned, smoked skin,
the front covered with woven porcupine quillwork. Sheath is quill-edged; cuff at top is
decorated with quillwork in zigzag-band
technique and has a compact fringe of metal
cones and red hair. Strap is of thongs, the
sections quill-wrapped in netted technique alternating with simple wrapping of paired thongs.
Colours are red, orange, blue and yellow on
strap; green, blue, yellow and white on sheath.
Sewn with sinew.
L. case 22.5 cm; L. carrying strap 66 cm
Eastern Great Lakes, before 1800

Speyer Collection; formerly in the James Hooper
Collection, England.
NMM III–X–239

67

Pouch
Made from tanned, black-dyed skin. Flap-type
closure. Porcupine-quill decoration consists of
one-quill edging and zigzag-band and simple
line techniques on front. Flap and bottom edges
are trimmed with opaque white beads and with
tassels of metal cones, red-dyed hair and cylindrical white and blue glass beads.
Carrying strap consists of 16 thongs bound
together in pairs with quills; at top of strap and
where the ends are joined to bag, thongs are
interwoven in netted technique. Thong ends
terminate in the same type of tassels as on the
pouch.
Quill colours in the pouch are orange, yellow,
black and white, and in the carrying strap are
black, red and white. Sewing and quillwork are
with sinew.
L. pouch w/o fringe 21 cm; L. carrying strap 117 cm
Ottawa type, c. 1780

*Speyer Collection; formerly in the collection of Sir John
Caldwell (see No. 21).*
NMM III-M-3

68

Pouch
Made from tanned, smoked skin in two pieces,
with two bands of woven porcupine quillwork
attached to pocket front. A compact fringe of
looped, quill-wrapped thongs is attached along
lower edge of each quill-woven band. Pouch is
edged in single-quill technique. Quill colours
are natural white, and red, blue, yellow and
brown. Sewn with sinew.
L. 27 cm
Cree type, before 1840

*Speyer Collection; formerly in the James Hooper Collec-
tion, England.*
NMM III-D-566

69

Knife and Sheath
Sheath is of tanned and smoked skin, with
edging of opaque white glass beads, porcupine
quills, and paired tassels of metal cones and red-
dyed hair. Front is decorated with broad quills
wrapped around two vertically-placed splints
(probably birch bark), with smaller quills in
contrasting colours interwoven at right angles.
Sinew-sewn.
Knife has iron blade set in wooden handle,
which is wrapped with tanned skin and then
with quills. Smaller quills interwoven at right
angles, as on sheath face. At top are two tassels
of metal cones and red-dyed hair.
L. sheath 22.5 cm; L. knife 28 cm
Mohawk-Iroquois type, late eighteenth century

*Speyer Collection; formerly in the collection of the Earl
of Warwick, Warwick Castle.*
NMM III-I-1323

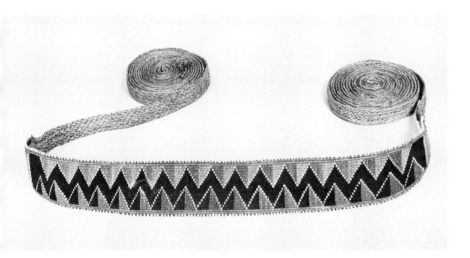

0

urden Strap
Made from Indian hemp, with moose-hair false
embroidery and edging of white glass beads on
forehead portion. This part is worked in twined
weave; at ends of woven area, warp strands are
braided, forming long tie-strings. Moose-hair
colours are orange, blue, black and white.
, 5.0 m; centre section 51 cm
Iroquois, before 1775

*Speyer Collection; formerly in the James Hooper Collec-
tion, England.*
NMM III-I-1230

71

Container
Made from birch bark seamed with spruce root.
Rim reinforced with wooden splints and bound
with roots, some left natural and others dyed
purple. Thong carrying strap. The dark inner
bark is on the outside of the basket, and designs
were created by scraping this away to expose the
lighter bark beneath.
L. 26.4 cm; H. 20.1 cm
Tête-de-Boule, before 1928

*Collected by G. D. T. Pickering at Manowan, Quebec,
in 1928*
NMM III-P-1

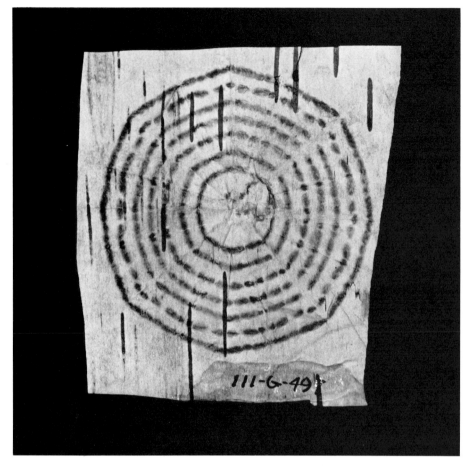

72

Bitten-Bark Pattern
Very thin inner birch bark, which has been
folded and bitten to produce design of
concentric circles.
4.7 × 5.0 cm
Northern Ojibwa, 1879

Collected by R. Bell from F. Richards at New Bruns-
wick House on Brunswick Lake, Ontario, in 1879
NMM III-G-497

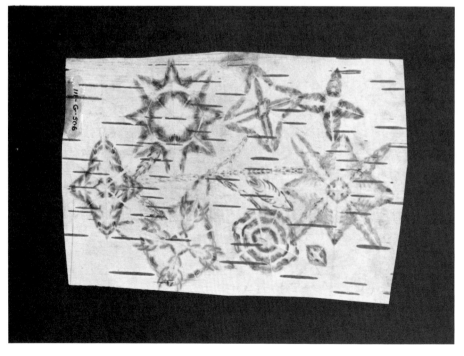

73

Bitten-Bark Patterns
Rectangle of thin inner birch bark that has been
folded and bitten to produce eight distinct
designs.
12.5 × 8.5 cm
Northern Ojibwa, 1879

Collected by R. Bell from F. Richards at New Bruns-
wick House on Brunswick Lake, Ontario, in 1879
NMM III-G-506

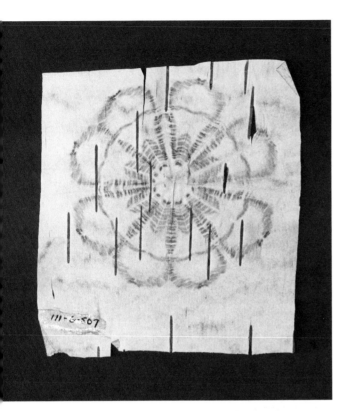

74

Bitten-Bark Pattern
Rectangle of very thin inner birch bark that has
been folded and bitten to produce floral pattern.
7.5 × 7.0 cm
Northern Ojibwa, 1879

Collected by R. Bell from F. Richards at New Bruns-
wick House on Brunswick Lake, Ontario, in 1879
NMM III-G-507

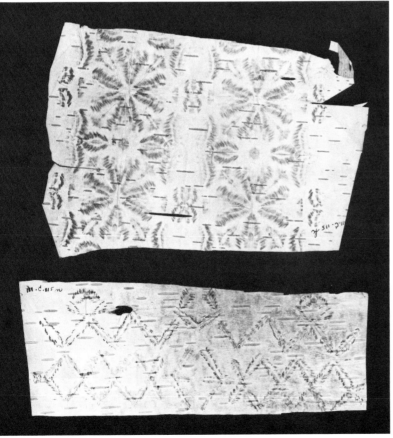

75

Bitten-Bark Patterns
Two pieces of very thin inner birch bark that
have been folded and bitten to produce designs.
Upper 16 × 11 cm; lower 17.5 × 6.5 cm
Montagnais, 1912

Collected by F. G. Speck at lac Saint-Jean, Quebec,
in 1912
NMM III-C-115k, n

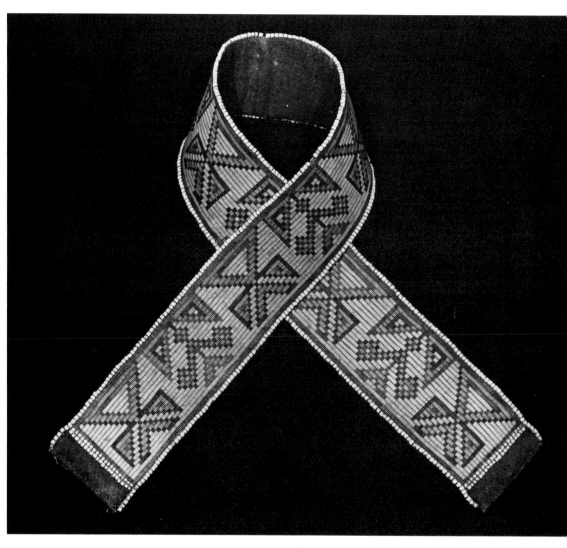

76

Belt
Broad band, 21 lanes deep, of woven porcupine
quillwork backed with birch bark and red
stroud. Edging of opaque white glass beads.
Quill colours are white, yellow, red and green.
L. 81.5 cm
Swampy Cree, before 1840

Speyer Collection; formerly in the collection of Fred
North, London.
NMM III–D–567

Moccasins

Each is made from a single piece of tanned, smoked skin seamed vertically at heel and gathered down centre front. Front seam and ankle flaps are covered with loom-woven quill-work, and edged with quills in zigzag-band technique. Ankle flaps are edged with fringe of metal cones and red hair; similar tassels, paired, are attached on moccasin fronts. Quill colours are white, blue, red, dark brown and yellow. Sewn with thong and string.

26 cm

Huron type, c. 1780

Speyer Collection; formerly in the collection of Sir John Caldwell (see No. 21).

CMM III-H-432

78

Pouch (colour plate, p. 54)
Made from tanned, black-dyed skin and
decorated with porcupine quillwork in three
techniques: edging, simple line stitch, and zigz
band. Three thunderbird motifs on lower fron
Opaque white glass beads incorporated in
edging. Tassels of metal cones and red hair.
Top edge of back bound with silk ribbon. Qui
colours are white, red, green and brownish
black. Sinew-sewn.
Carrying strap is of Indian hemp in twined
weave, decorated with moose-hair false embro
dery in orange, blue, yellow and white, Asymmetrical design treatment. Strap is edged with
opaque white glass beads. At strap ends, hemp
strands are quill-wrapped (white with transver
sections in red), and terminate in tassels of me
cones and red hair.
Bag 22 cm square; L. carrying strap w/o fringe 97 c
Eastern Ojibwa type, c. 1780

Speyer Collection; formerly in the collection of Sir Joh
Caldwell (see No. 21).
NMM III-G-828

9

Bag

Twined, made in one piece from red and black
woollen yarns and natural cotton string. The
faces differ. On one there is a panel of alternating black hourglass motifs and lozenges between
striped panels obliquely barred in red and black;
on the other is a panel of black lozenges
between similar barred and striped panels. Red
wool and string band around top. Free warp-
ends twisted and braided to form a firm edge.
W. 59 cm
Winnebago, second half of nineteenth century

*Acquired from the American Museum of Natural
History, New York, in 1925*
NMM III–O–2

80

Pouch
Made from black-dyed tanned skin, and
decorated with porcupine quillwork in three
techniques: edging, simple line, and zigzag ban
Two thunderbird motifs on front; cross motifs
on flap. Tassels of quill-wrapped thongs, metal
cones and red hair. Quill colours are white,
orange, yellow and brownish black. Sinew-
sewn, repaired with commercial thread.
Carrying strap missing.
W. 25 cm
Eastern Ojibwa or Ottawa type, 1800

Speyer Collection; formerly in the Greatorex Collectio
Whitechapel Museum, London, and later in the Jame
Hooper Collection, England.
NMM III-G-829

ittens
ade from tanned, unsmoked (white) caribou
n. Set-in thumb. Lining of fine white skin,
d a skin binding (originally furred) around
ist. Painted designs in red and in deep yellow
m fish glue that has yellowed with age. Sewn
th cotton thread.
26 cm
skapi, before 1840

yer Collection; formerly in the collection of Princess
érèse of Bavaria in the Staatliches Museum für
lkerkunde, Munich.
MM III-B-593

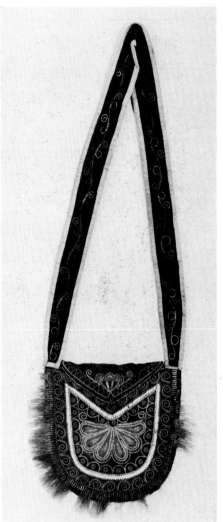

82

Pouch
Made from black-dyed tanned skin; pouch back
of smoked skin. Strap is backed and edged with
beige cotton. Pouch front is outlined with
compact fringe of metal cylinders and red-dyed
deer hair. Pouch and strap are decorated with
moose-hair appliqué in simple line stitch;
colours are orange, blue, white and green. Single
lane of white porcupine quillwork in zigzag-
band technique. Button formed from silk-
wrapped pebble. Sewn with commercial thread.
L. pouch w/o fringe 16.5 cm; L. carrying strap 85 cm
Huron, before 1829

Speyer Collection; formerly in the collection of the Duke
of Gotha.
NMM III-H-426

83

Pipe Bowl
Bird effigy type, of mottled grey stone, with
carved bird facing smoker, its breast forming t
bowl. Bird has crest, and other details are deep
incised.
L. 12 cm
Cherokee type, late prehistoric

*Acquired from a dealer in Antwerp in 1972. Label
attached to base reads: "Union Co., S.C."*
NMM N-I-6

84

Pipe Bowl
Made from blackened grey stone. Bowl is in the
form of a human head facing the smoker.
Arching up from base to back of bowl is a
carved dragon-like figure, with small limbs in
low relief on sides. The front of the base is
broken off and missing.
H. 8.5 cm
Eastern Ojibwa type, 1840

*Speyer Collection; formerly in the collection of Fred
North, London.*
NMM III-G-832

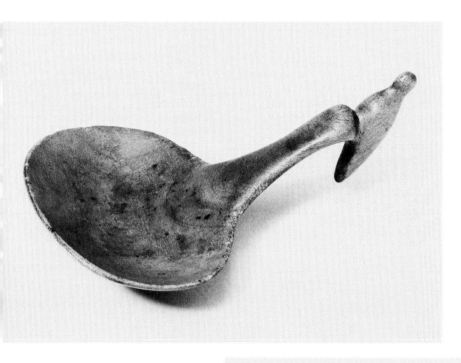

oon
rved from a single piece of wood. Handle end
ved into bird shape, tail of which forms a
ckward-pointing hook so that the spoon can
hung on the edge of a bowl.
15.3 cm
quois type, nineteenth century

quired from a dealer in New York in 1975
MM III–I–1365

86

Pipe
Pottery, with bowl in shape of human face
facing smoker. Back of bowl decorated with
incised lines and dots.
L. 14 cm
St. Lawrence Iroquois, c. 1550

Collected by W. J. Wintemberg at the Roebuck archae-
ological site, Grenville County, Ontario, in 1912
NMM VIII–F–12005

87

Headdress
Cap made from tanned skin, tapered to a fringed point at back and seamed down centre crown. Decoration of parallel lines pressed into the surface: on one side these are vertical and unpainted; on the other side, horizontal and either unpainted or painted black and red. Broad band of tanned skin is attached around rim, decorated with quill-wrapped strips of rawhide. Trapezoidal tabs of tanned, smoked skin and red-dyed feathers are inserted between band and cap; feathers are stitched to base of vegetable-fibre thread. Large peacock feathers were originally also secured here. Tassels of metal cones, quill-wrapped thongs, and hair. Thong tie-strings. Quill colours are orange, yellow, white and dark brown. Sewn with cotton thread.
L. 35 cm
Great Lakes, eighteenth century

Speyer Collection; formerly in the collection of the Ea of Warwick, Warwick Castle.
NMM III-X-241

88

Moccasins
Made from tanned, black-dyed skin. Basically one-piece construction, with small additions to ankle flaps. Heel seams and fronts are decorated with porcupine quillwork in two techniques: zigzag band (using up to three different colours of quills) and simple line. Quill colours are orange, turquoise, yellow and natural white. Sinew-sewn.
L. 25.5 cm
Ojibwa, 1830

Speyer Collection; formerly in the Schwarz Collection, Vienna (see No. 66).
NMM III-G-831

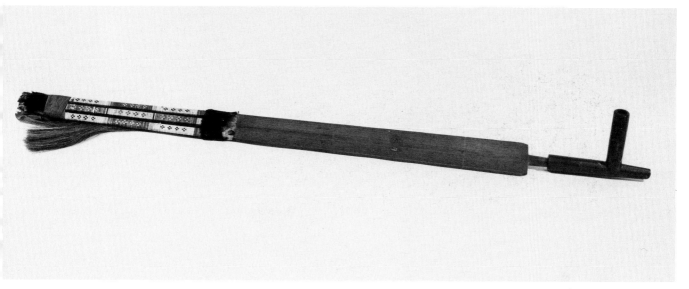

pe

bow-type bowl, with anterior projection, made
m red pipestone (catlinite) smoothly finished.
at wooden stem with openwork carving
rming three longitudinal sections near mouth.
ese sections are quill-wrapped, with smaller
ills in contrasting colours interwoven at right
gles to create open cross designs. At either
d of quill-decorated portion, stem is wrapped
th duck skin and red silk ribbon. A hank of
een-dyed horsehair is attached under bird-
in wrapping. Quill colours are green, red,
llow, white and dark brown.
pipe 14.5 cm; L. stem 80 cm
stern Sioux, 1860s

eyer Collection; formerly in the collection of
A. Lichtenberger, who acquired it from the
innesota Sioux before 1867.
MM V-E-289

90

Pipe Bowl
Made from black stone, highly polished.
Scalloped bottom edge, keel-shaped base,
curved line and dot incisions on both sides of
base. Perforation through base, presumably for
the attachment of ornaments or of thongs for
securing bowl to stem.
H. 11 cm
Ojibwa type, late eighteenth century

Speyer Collection; formerly in the collection of Sir
Walter Scott, 1771–1832.
NMM III-G-833

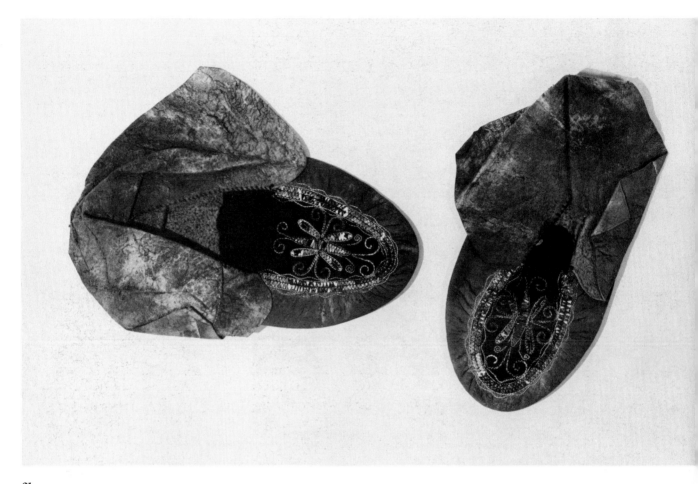

91

Moccasins
Made from tanned, smoked skin, with vamp of
black-dyed skin. Vamp is decorated with porcupine quillwork in zigzag-band and simple line
techniques, and white moose-hair in oversewn-
line technique. Quill colours are blue, green,
orange-red and white. Sewn with cotton thread.
L. 23 cm
Huron type, before 1825

Speyer Collection; formerly in the collection of the Duke
von Coburg-Gotha.
NMM III–H–433

92

Man's Coat
Made from tanned caribou skin. Flared skirt
with triangular inset in back. Designs painted in
deep yellow (from fish glue that has yellowed
with age) and in red, blue and blue-green;
design elements include parallel lines, flattened
double curve, triangles, cross-hatching and
dotted lines. Sinew-sewn.
L. 105 cm
Naskapi, before 1770

Speyer Collection; formerly in the collection of the
Grand Duke of Baden.
NMM III-B-589

93

Pouch
Made from smoked, tanned skin, with drawstring laced through top. Pendant strands of
cylindrical black and white glass beads on
commercial string, ending in tassels of dyed red
hair and tin cones. Fringe of same components
along bottom edge. Partial edging of green and
white glass beads. Both sides decorated with
porcupine quillwork in zigzag-band technique
in white, red, green, yellow and black. Along
base of pouch is single oversewn line of green
moose-hair embroidery. Sewn with commercial
thread.
L. w/o fringe 17.5 cm
Iroquois, before 1790

Speyer Collection
NMM III-I-1324

94

Moccasins
Made from tanned, smoked skin decorated with
porcupine quills in zigzag-band and simple line
techniques. Downturned ankle flaps edged with
pink silk ribbon and white seed beads. Sewn
with cotton thread and sinew.
L. 24 cm
Seneca type, c. 1830

*Speyer Collection; formerly in the Staatliches Museum
für Völkerkunde, Frankfurt, West Germany. According
to a note glued to the sole, they were acquired from
Indians in Buffalo, New York, and in 1836 donated to
the Senckenbergischen Gesellschaft, Frankfurt, by Mrs.
Sophie Kraus, née Rüppell.*
NMM III-I-1309

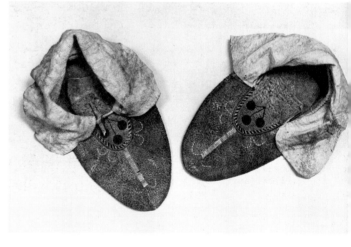

95

Moccasins
Made from heavy tanned, smoked skin, with
ankle flaps of unsmoked skin. Double-layer
vamp decorated with horsehair piping and with
porcupine quillwork in three techniques: four-
quill diamond, simple line, and zigzag band.
Piping is in yellow, brown and red; quill colours
are bright pink and blue. Sewn with cotton
thread and sinew.
L. 25.5 cm
Cree type, early twentieth century

*Acquired from a dealer who had purchased them in
Paris in 1949*
NMM III-D-569

97

Woman's Dress (colour plate, p. 55)
Side-fold type, with downturned yoke; made from single tanned, unsmoked skin. Seamed up the side, and edges cut into fringe. Quill-wrapped fringes attached around lower edges of yoke, at one shoulder, and around hem; quill-wrapped thongs are secured transversely by ties of sinew and vegetable fibre. Lower skirt is encircled by a lane of lazy-stitch beading, edged with a line of red porcupine quills in sawtooth technique. Pendant pairs of quill-wrapped thongs are attached at intervals along quilled lane. Below this the skirt is painted with ochre-orange blotches; similar painting occurs on the yoke. There is a short lane of lazy-stitch beading shoulder.

wing is with sinew. Thongs are sewn on the side top for fastening the dress over the shoulders. Bead colours are dull turquoise and white. Quill colours are red, blue, white, yellow, pink and brownish purple.

w. fringe 128 cm
Plains Cree type, 1840

Speyer Collection; acquired from Commodore Walzer, Salisbury, England.
NMM V-A-439

Man's Shirt
Made from two tanned deer or antelope skins. Quillworked bands bordered by deep turquoise-blue pony beads are attached to each sleeve; one runs from neck to sleeve end, the other at right angles over shoulder. Quills are applied in zigzag-band technique. Large rosettes quilled in band technique on skin discs are sewn to centre front and back. Bands of red stroud with white, blue and green glass beadwork are attached at neck. Painted decoration of parallel lines in dark brown on sleeves, and of lines and dots on upper front and back in dark brown against a yellow background. Locks of dark-brown and yellow horsehair, each bound at base with pericardium and white quills and attached to a thong strung with a large blue glass bead, are fastened along edge of quilled band on one sleeve; down the other sleeve, tassels are of twisted ermine skin bound at base with red stroud and pericardium, and similarly strung with thongs and blue beads. Sewn with sinew. Quill colours are yellow, red, orange, white and blue; brown maidenhair fern is also used.

L. through middle: 89 cm
Blackfoot, 1840

Speyer Collection; acquired from Commodore Walzer, Salisbury, England.
NMM V-B-413

98

Moccasins
Made from tanned, smoked skin, and seamed
around outer edge of foot. Added tongue and
ankle flap. Porcupine-quill appliqué in several
techniques: around curved edge of foot, three
woven rows of quills, with warp strands knotted
into the skin; on front, a coiled rosette of quill-
wrapped sinew plus quillwork in band
technique; on ankle flaps, plaited and zigzag-
band techniques. Ankle-flap fringe of quill-
wrapped thongs linked transversely with sinew
line strung with blue glass beads; brass cone
jinglers. Quill colours are white, brown, blue
and yellow; brown maidenhair fern is also used.
Small amount of red paint at toe. Sinew-sewn.
L. 25.5 cm
Mandan, before 1840

Speyer Collection
NMM V-H-1

99

Bridle Trim
Side pieces and rosettes made from quill-
decorated tanned skin backed with red stroud,
which has been cut into rectangular notches
along protruding edges. Top piece is woven
quillwork, edged at either end with row of
yellow and white glass beads. Now-fragmentary
fringe of quill-wrapped thongs, tin cones and
blue wool. Quill colours are yellow, white, red,
brownish black and blue.
L. sides 36 cm
Plains Cree type, 1840

*Speyer Collection; acquired from a London dealer
in 1963.*
NMM V-A-440

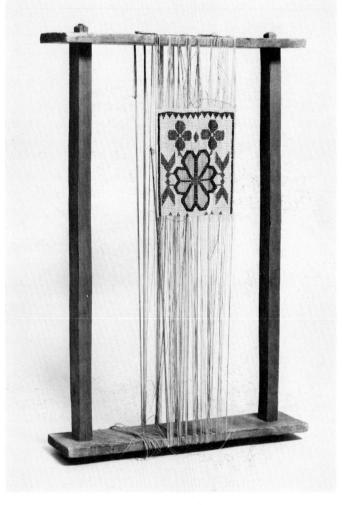

101

Woven Beadwork on Loom
Oblong wooden frame strung with warp of linen
thread. Weft also of linen thread, with designs
in blue (2 shades), red, green and clear seed
beads against background of white beads.
Design is conventionalized rose, according to
Lyford (1953: pl. 87).
L. 48.5 cm
Ojibwa type, twentieth century

Collector unknown
NMM III-G-820

0

elt
eadwoven band of black and white pony
eads, with triangular tabs of tanned skin sewn
t ends. Technique is square weave; warp is
ouble-strand yellow-brown wool (respun from
welled cloth), and weft is double-strand cotton
read. Non-repeating designs are worked down
iddle of band.
. *beadwork 98 cm*
astern Great Lakes, c. 1780

*peyer Collection; formerly in the collection of Sir John
aldwell (see No. 21).
MM III-X-242*

102

Sash
Finger-woven of hard-textured, tightly-spun
woollen yarn, with white pony beads interwoven to produce zigzag-line patterns. Colour is
pink, with narrow band of blue-green along
both edges. At ends, warp strands are braided,
then twisted and knotted to form fringe. A few
strands of the fringe are also braided, and are
strung with white beads.
L. w/o fringe 122 cm
Eastern Great Lakes, c. 1780

Speyer Collection; formerly in the collection of Sir John
Caldwell (see No. 21).
NMM III–X–243

3

an's Shirt
inted cotton cloth, hand-sewn with cotton
ead. Ruffle-edged opening at centre front, and
ffled cuffs. Downturned collar. Ties at neck
d sleeve-ends.
at middle 92 cm
stern Great Lakes, c. 1780

eyer Collection; formerly in the collection of Sir John
ldwell (see No. 21).
MM III-X-244

104

Netting Needle
Carved from single piece of birch. Used to carry
twine in making nets.
L. 21.5 cm
Western Woods Cree, before 1939

Collected by D. Leechman at Long Lake, Alberta
(Onion Lake Agency), in 1939
NMM V-A-237

Fish Net
Made from commercial twine, with rope around
outer edge. Used in summer and fall for catch-
ing pike and sturgeon.
L. 29.5 m
Swampy Cree, 1967

Collected at Moose Factory, Ontario, in 1973. Made
by Sophia Small.
NMM III-D-429

Net Gauge
Thin rectangular piece of wood with rounded
edges on the two longest sides.
5.5 × 4.5 cm
Tête-de-Boule, before 1912

Collected by F. G. Speck on the rivière Saint-Maurice,
Quebec, in 1912
NMM III-P-2

105

Knife
Steel blade set in wooden handle. Handle is
covered with tanned skin, and wrapped with
orange and white porcupine quills secured with
sinew. At handle end are four tassels of quill-
wrapped thongs, metal cones, and red-dyed
hair. Manufacturer's mark on blade.
L. 28.5 cm
Iroquois type, late eighteenth century

Speyer Collection; formerly in the collection of the Earl
of Warwick, Warwick Castle.
NMM III-I-1325

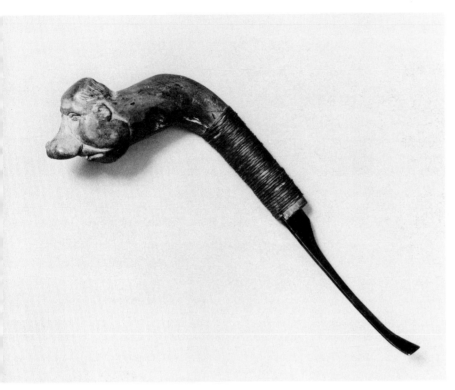

106

Crooked Knife
Blade made from iron file sharpened along one
edge, with distal end slightly curved. Blade is
fitted into wooden handle, the join wrapped
with sinew. Handle end is carved into the carica-
ture of a man's head.
L. 26.4 cm
Abenaki, before 1914

Collected by F. G. Speck at Pierreville, Quebec,
in 1914
NMM III-J-45

107

Pipe-Tomahawk
Wooden shaft, elliptical in cross-section, shaped
at end to form mouthpiece. Handle decorated
with burn markings and with inlays and encir-
cling bands of white metal. English-style iron
head combining bowl and hatchet-type blade.
L. 63 cm
Seneca, 1800

Speyer Collection; formerly in the collection of the Duke
of Gotha.
NMM III-I-1315

108

Pipe-Tomahawk

French-style iron blade and bowl combination with openwork-heart motif; one curling flange broken off at base. Wooden handle decorated with brass tacks and by burning with a hot file. Sheath of tanned skin over lower handle, with lazy-stitch beading and a beaded triangular pendant that has a long fringe of twisted and knotted thongs, every three strands wrapped with quills near base of triangle. Pony beads are white, dull pink, dark blue, red and yellow.
L. w/o pendant 64 cm
Teton Sioux, c. 1850

Speyer Collection; formerly in a museum in Neuchâtel, Switzerland. An attached label reads: " 'Tomahawk' . . . de la tribu des Brules Sioux dans le Wyoming Territory. Le chef de cette tribu est le célèbre 'Red Cloud' . . ."
NMM V-E-272

109

War Club

Gunstock type, with broad double-edged iron blade inserted in wooden handle. Handle studded with brass tacks, and painted red with yellow border trim and floral motifs. Written on handle in black ink: "Missouri, M. Z. Wied".
L. 73 cm
Missouri, 1833

Speyer Collection; formerly in the collection of Prince Maximilian zu Wied (see No. 18).
NMM V-N-3

110

Brooch
Large silver brooch with engraved and
openwork designs. Pin missing. Maker's mark
"J T", engraved on front, refers to Jonathan
Tyler, a Montreal silversmith who produced
silver for the Indian trade up to 1817.
Diam. 20.8 cm
Algonkin, before 1817

*Found by Mrs. M. Buckshot at Eagle Rapids, 30 miles
northwest of Gracefield, Quebec, on the Gatineau River
in 1916*
NMM III-L-195

111

Headband
Broad, thin silver band, with perforated
diamonds, triangles and arrowheads and fine
zigzag-line engraving. Lower edge is scalloped,
and has small dangling hearts attached. Maker's
mark "SM", in cartouche at one end, refers to
Salomon Marion, Montreal silversmith, whose
working dates are c. 1818–32.
L. 60 cm; H. 7 cm
Algonkin, c. 1818–32

*Collected by E. Sapir from Catherine Michel at
Maniwaki, Quebec, in 1912*
NMM III-L-17

112

Headdress
Rectangle of black silk folded into triangular
head scarf. At top are attached small silver
brooches of a simple disc variety. Around face,
ball and pendant-cone type earrings for pierced
ears are attached to brooches.
Diam. of brooches 2.1 cm
Eastern Great Lakes, c. 1780

Speyer Collection; formerly in the collection of Sir John
Caldwell (see No. 21).
NMM III–X–245

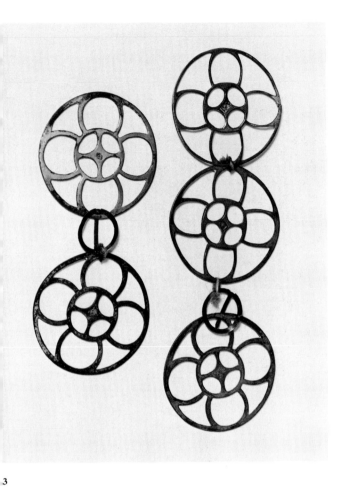

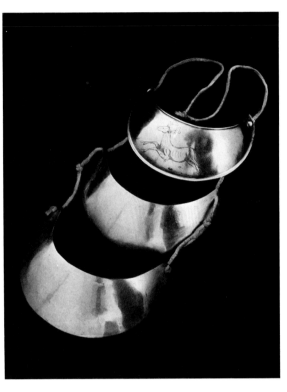

114

Breast-Plates
Three silver gorgets, linked together with
knotted thong. Upper gorget has maker's mark
"RC" (see No. 113), and is engraved with the
figure of a deer. The other two gorgets are of
simple hammered silver.
W. (largest) 12.5 cm; W. (smallest) 8.5 cm
Eastern Great Lakes, c. 1780

*Speyer Collection; formerly in the collection of Sir
John Caldwell (see No. 21).*
NMM III-X-247

3

r Pendants
vo ear pendants, one with two silver discs with
enwork designs, the other with three discs;
ere are two small silver brooches linking the
scs. Two of the discs have fine zigzag-line and
t engraving on face. Each disc has maker's
ark in centre: two have "I*S", referring to
nas Schindler, of Quebec, who produced
verwork between 1779 and 1802; three have
.C", referring to Robert Cruikshank, of
ontreal, who worked between 1779 and 1809.
am. 5.8 cm
stern Great Lakes, c. 1780

eyer Collection; formerly in the collection of Sir John
ldwell (see No. 21).
MM III-X-246

115

Armband
Wide silver band with raised rims. Fine zigzag-
line engraving on face, in form of Maltese cross.
L. 25 cm; W. 7.2 cm
Iroquois, before 1792

Speyer Collection
NMM III-I-1326

117

Sash
Tightly finger-woven of hard-textured woollen yarn. Made in four interlocked bands; colours are green, red, purple and yellow. At ends, long fringe is formed from warp ends twisted together, then knotted.
L. w/o fringe 134 cm
Great Lakes Algonkians, c. 1780

Speyer Collection; formerly in the collection of Sir John Caldwell (see No. 21).
NMM III-X-261

116

Arrow Sash
A *ceinture fléchée* finger-woven from tightly twisted, hard-textured woollen yarn. Pattern consists of red core flanked by parallel zigzags in alternating beige, dark blue, light blue, red, yellow and green. At both ends, strands are braided, then twisted to form fringe.
L. w/o fringe 187 cm
Lorette Huron, early nineteenth century

Acquired from Cyrille Bastien at Village-des-Hurons, Quebec, in 1974. Formerly the property of Maurice Sebastien (Ahgniolen), 1823-1897, Grand Chief of the Lorette Hurons.
NMM III-H-434

118

Breechclout
Made of blue stroud, the middle portion backed with unbleached cotton. Ends decorated with edging of white glass beads and appliqués of silk ribbon and wool tape in green, mauve, and deep pink. Sewing is with cotton thread and indigenous vegetable fibres.
L. 127 cm
Eastern Great Lakes, c. 1780

Speyer Collection; formerly in the collection of Sir John Caldwell (see No. 21).
NMM III-X-248

occasin Vamps
ade of commercially tanned skin, beaded
rtion backed with double layer of paper.
adwork designs first marked with pencil, then
ads attached with overlay stitch, using cotton
read. Bead colours are red, yellow, green and
nslucent light green.
15 cm
stern Sioux, 1970

ollected at the Sioux Valley Indian Reserve,
anitoba, in 1970
MM V-E-246

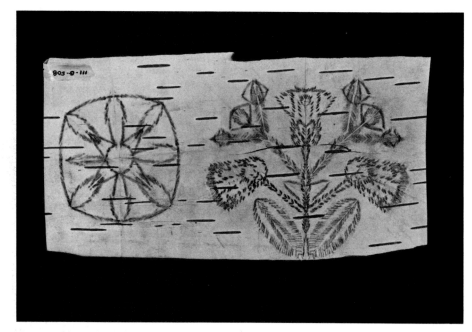

120

Bitten-Bark Patterns
Very thin birch bark that has been folded and
bitten to produce two separate designs.
14 × 7.5 cm
Northern Ojibwa, 1879

*Collected by R. Bell from F. Richards at New Bruns-
wick House on Brunswick Lake, Ontario, in 1879*
NMM III-G-508

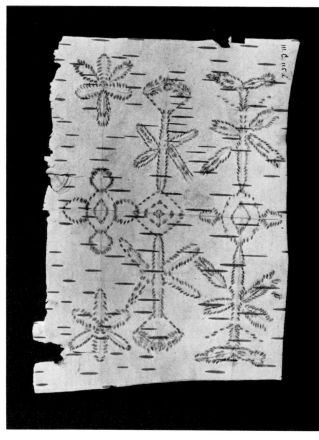

121

Bitten-Bark Patterns
Very thin birch bark that has been folded and
bitten to produce five different designs.
17.5 × 13 cm
Montagnais, 1912

*Collected by F.G. Speck at lac Saint-Jean, Quebec,
in 1912*
NMM III-C-115i

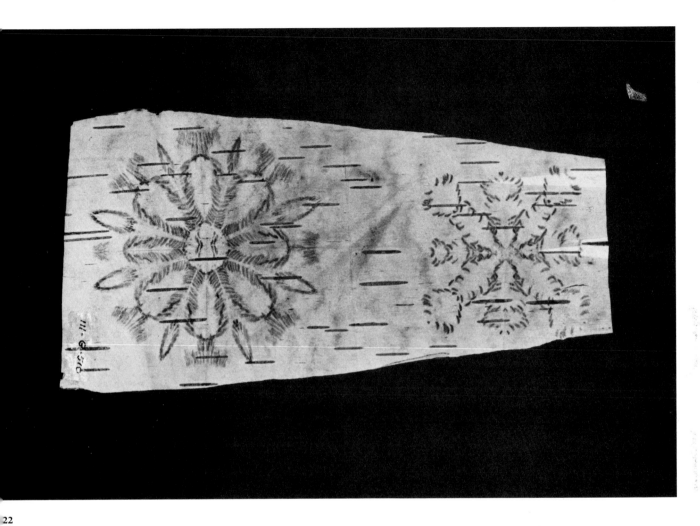

22

Bitten-Bark Patterns
Very thin birch bark, folded and bitten to
produce two separate designs.
3.5 × 6.5 cm
Northern Ojibwa, 1879

Collected by R. Bell from F. Richards at New Brunswick House on Brunswick Lake, Ontario, in 1879
NMM III-G-510

123

Canoe Model with Four Dolls and Equipment
Birch-bark canoe with wood sheathing, ribs and
crossbars. Sewn with split roots; gunwales
bound with roots, with white moose hair interwoven at right angles. Seams sealed with spruce
gum. Curving designs painted on exterior in red,
white, green and black paint, with series of dots
outlining motifs. Crossbars and gunwales are
painted red.
Two male and two female dolls. Heads and arms
moulded of beeswax, bodies of stuffed cotton
cloth. All wear trade-cloth clothing, metal
armbands, and necklaces of red, blue and white
glass beads. One male figure wears eared
headdress of red stroud decorated with yellow
silk ribbon and beads. Moccasins of tanned
skin. Eyes are inlays of black and white claylike
material. Lips are painted red, and facial
markings are in black and red.

Accessories include wooden models of a
powder-horn, a liquor bottle, two guns, a keg,
and a toboggan with red-painted designs, as well
as a small stuffed dog of brown woollen cloth.
There are four wooden paddles with handles
painted red; designs on blades are painted in
red, black, blue, green and yellow.
L. canoe 72 cm; H. largest doll 25 cm
Malecite type, c. 1800

Speyer Collection; acquired from a London dealer.
NMM III–E–311

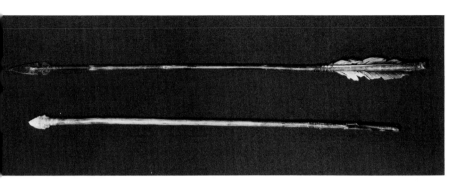

125

Arrow
At top, a wooden shaft with brass point. Two split and trimmed feathers. Shaft and sinew lashings painted red.
L. 55.5 cm
Eastern Woodlands, nineteenth century

Speyer Collection
NMM III-X-260

4

rrow
t bottom, a wooden shaft with triangular point
•ked from milk glass. Feathering of two split
•d trimmed hawk feathers. Sinew lashings.
•inting in red, green and black at shaft ends.
49.5 cm
•stern Woodlands, nineteenth century

eyer Collection
MM III-X-249

126

Knife and Sheath (colour plate, p. 56)
Knife has broad double-edged steel blade set in wooden handle, which is bound with quill-wrapped thongs and has a fringe of thongs strung with glass beads and terminating in woollen tassels.
Sheath is of thin wood with covering of tanned skin. A transverse bar of skin-covered wood is attached across the front, at top; this is faced with strip of woven porcupine quillwork, and has fringes of red stroud and bead-strung thongs. Painting on sheath is in red and black.

Carrying strap of interwoven red-stained thongs and glass beads. Sewn with sinew and commercial thread.
Quill colours are white, yellow and red; beads are multicoloured.
L. knife 29.5 cm; L. sheath 24 cm
Swampy Cree type, eighteenth century

Speyer Collection; formerly in the collection of the Earl of Warwick, Warwick Castle.
NMM III-D-568

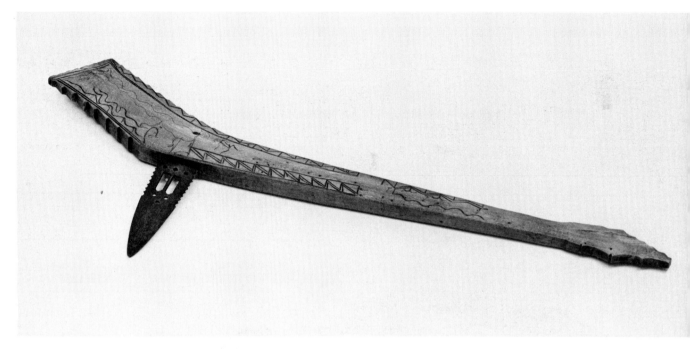

127

War Club
Gun-stock type, of wood with steel point. Flat-sided handle, ridged slightly along middle. Incised designs include an underworld panther and a running human figure.
L. 68 cm
Central Ojibwa type, 1800

Speyer Collection; formerly in the Greatorex Collection, Whitechapel Museum, London.
NMM III-G-834

128

War Club
Gunstock type, of heavy wood with iron point. Flat-sided handle ridged slightly along middle and painted in blue-black and red. Decorated with fringed red and gold woollen tape, green, red, gold and mauve woollen tape, and single eagle feather.
L. 84 cm
Winnebago, before 1835

Speyer Collection
NMM III-O-3

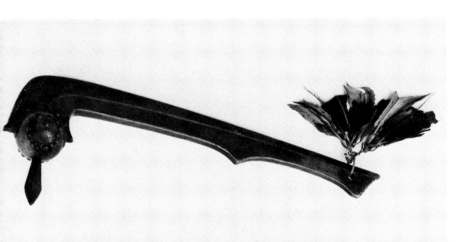

129

Club
Ball-headed type made from single piece of
wood, originally painted dark red over-all. Iron
point. Brass-tack decoration on head, and
deeply incised grooves along top of handle.
Painted green, yellow and red on head and at
top of handle. Tassel of cut feathers and red-
dyed horsehair attached to end of handle.
L. 62 cm
Eastern Plains Siouans, said to be of Omaha origin,
1800

Speyer Collection; originally in a private collection in
Scotland.
NMM V–X–395

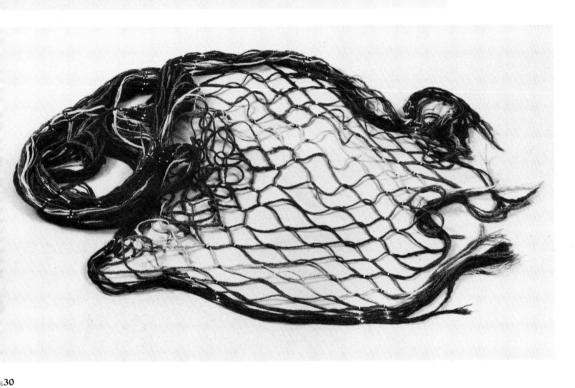

130

Sash
Forty strands of braided woollen yarn bound
together with porcupine quills in netted
technique. Wool colours are mauve, green, red
and yellow; quill colours are white, black, red
and green.
L. 2.56 m
Eastern Great Lakes, c. 1780

Speyer Collection; formerly in the collection of Sir John
Caldwell (see No. 21).
NMM III–X–250

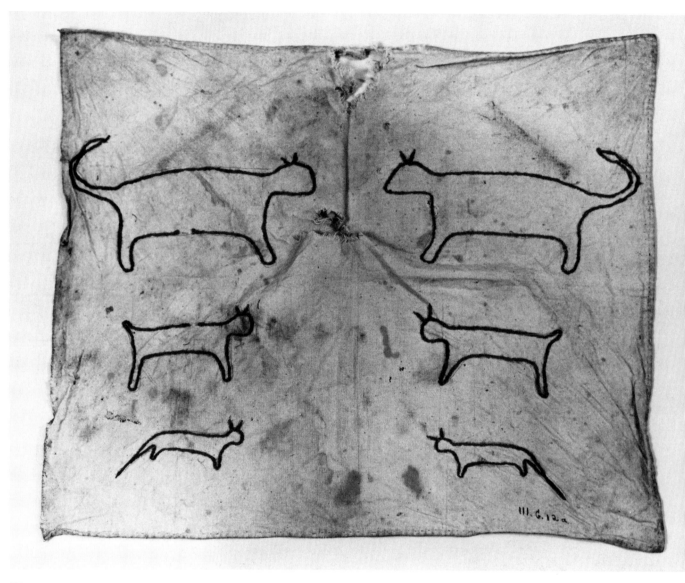

131

Ceremonial Cloth
Natural-coloured calico with three pairs of
animals outlined in red woollen yarn. Sewn with
cotton thread. Used in Medicine Lodge rituals.
55.5 × 47 cm
Ojibwa, before 1912

*Collected by A. B. Reagan at the Bois Fort Reserva-
tion, northern Minnesota, in 1912*
NMM III–G–12a

132

Leggings
Made from fine black wool broadcloth. Bottom
and flap edges bound with ribbon and decorated
with ribbon appliqué; colours are pink and blue,
orange and green. Ribbon ties at top.
L. 62 cm
Great Lakes, nineteenth century

Speyer Collection
NMM III-X-251

133

Moccasin Ankle-Flaps
Made from two pieces of black wool broadcloth,
decorated with ribbon appliqué. Remains of
bead trim around edges. Sewn and beaded with
silk thread.
L. 21 cm
Wyandot, before 1912

Collected by C. M. Barbeau from Mrs. Pipe Stannard
at the Wyandotte Reservation, Oklahoma, in 1912
NMM III-H-225

134

Pipe Bowl
Made of blackened greenish-grey stone,
decorated with deeply incised lines.
L. 8.2 cm
Eastern Canada, early nineteenth century

Speyer Collection
NMM III–X–252

135

Pipe Bowl
A large bowl of black stone decorated with
incised cross-hatching, holes and notching.
H. 13 cm
Blackfoot type, early nineteenth century

Speyer Collection; formerly in the collection of the
Methodist Missionary Society, London, and later in
the James Hooper Collection, England.
NMM V–B–422

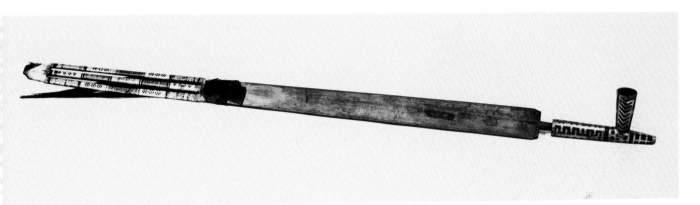

136

Calumet
Flat wooden stem with two longitudinal cutout sections. Porcupine-quill wrapping, with contrasting quills interwoven at right angles to produce cross motifs. Decorated with bird-skin wrappings, green ribbon bow, and red-dyed horsehair. Stem painted green. Quill colours are blue, red, yellow, white and brownish black. Bowl is of red catlinite, with extensive lead inlay.
L. stem 89 cm; L. bowl 16 cm
Yankton Sioux, before 1843

Speyer Collection; formerly in the collection of the Grand Duke of Baden.
NMM V-E-290

137

Pipe Bowl
Made of red catlinite with lead inlay. Human head with features in relief carved at end of anterior projection; trapezoidal crest in front of bowl.
L. 17.5 cm
Eastern Sioux type, early nineteenth century

Speyer Collection; formerly in the Linden-Museum, Stuttgart, West Germany.
NMM V-E-291

138

Pipe Bowl
Made from dull red catlinite, with tapered
anterior projection, and crest in front of bowl.
Lead inlay.
L. 17.5 cm
Minnesota Ojibwa type, early nineteenth century

Speyer Collection; formerly in the collection of the
Methodist Missionary Society, London.
NMM III-G-840

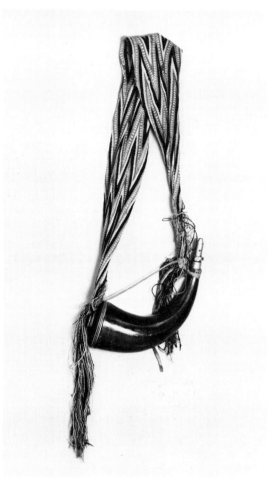

139

Sash
Finger-woven of woollen yarn in three interlocked bands, with white pony beads interwoven to outline arrow pattern. Pattern is
worked in olive-green and pale blue against a
red background.
L. w/o fringe 85 cm
Huron type, 1800

Speyer Collection; acquired from a London dealer.
NMM III-H-428

140

Powder-Horn with Sash
Sash is tightly finger-woven of hard-textured
woollen yarns. Yarn colours are red, black,
yellow, blue and white. At ends, strands are
twisted and knotted to form fringe. Tanned,
smoked thong attaches sash to horn.
Powder-horn is of non-Indian manufacture, with
wood and brass fittings.
L. horn 34 cm; L. sash w/o fringe 91 cm
Great Lakes Algonkians, c. 1780

Speyer Collection; formerly in the collection of Sir John
Caldwell (see No. 21).
NMM III-X-262

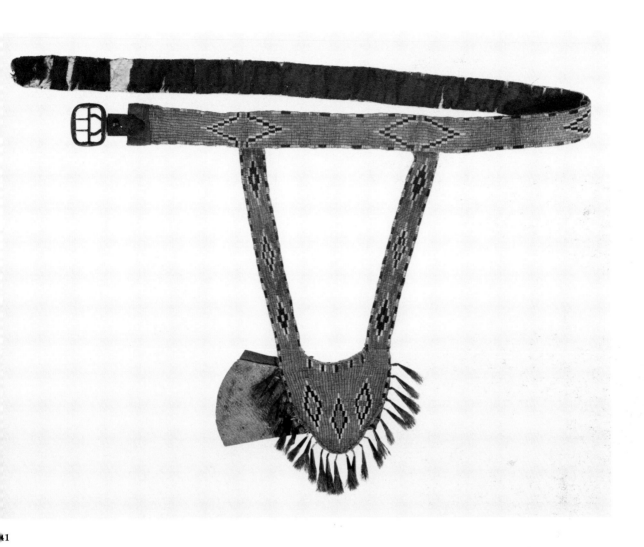

41

Sword Belt

Woven porcupine quillwork on warp and weft
of Indian hemp. Backed with beige and green
silk. On pendant, tassel fringe of brass cones
and red hair on hemp strings wrapped with
quills and silk thread. Small sleeve of red-dyed
commercially tanned leather attached across
back of pendant. Metal buckle of European
origin. Attached label, partly illegible, reads:
"balteus pro gladio confectus e pennis hystricis
americanae ab Indiana Iroquaea . . . D. D.
Guilielmo Johnson Baronetto Regi . . . New York
ono . . . propraetori . . ."
L. belt w/o buckle 113 cm; L. pendant w/o fringe 31 cm
Iroquois (Mohawk?), 1760–70

Speyer Collection; formerly in the collection of a king of
Bavaria, and acquired in 1913 by the Staatliches
Museum für Völkerkunde, Munich. Apparently origi-
nally acquired by Sir William Johnson.
MM III-I-1327

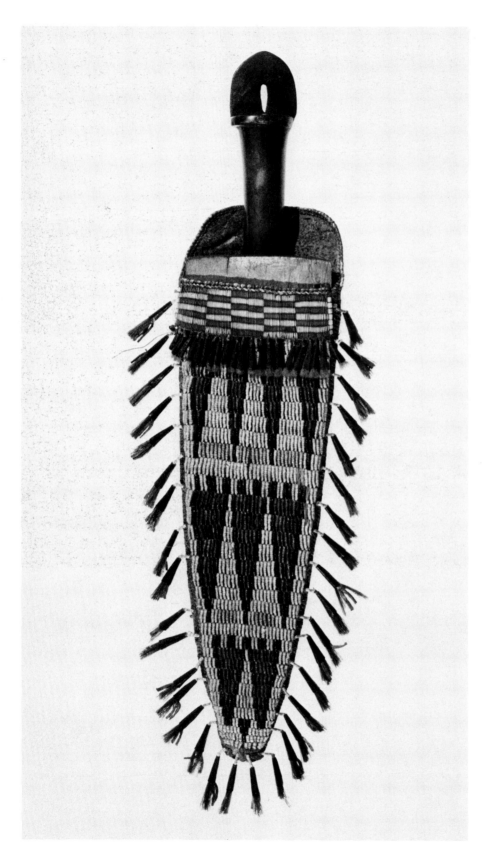

142

Knife and Sheath
Sheath of tanned, smoked skin, front covered
with porcupine quills in netted technique.
Attached at top is a strip of woven quills, with
line of white glass beads at either end. Fringes
quill-wrapped thongs, brass cones, and tassels
green wool or red hair. Single-quill edging.
Quill colours are reddish-brown, dark brown,
yellow, green and white. Sinew-sewn. Sheath
lined with birch bark.
Knife has single-edged iron blade and horn
handle.
L. knife 31 cm; L. sheath w/o fringe 30 cm
Northern Ojibwa type, c. 1800

Speyer Collection; acquired from a London dealer.
NMM III-G-835

43

Man's Coat (colour plate, p. 57)

For summer wear. Made from finely-tanned caribou skin, sewn with sinew and decorated with pressed and painted designs in red, green, and deep yellow derived from fish glue that has yellowed with age. Three triangular insets in lower back of skirt. Broad cuffs; rectangular downturned collar attached at neck back.

105 cm

Naskapi, early nineteenth century

Speyer Collection; formerly in a German museum.

CMM III–B–590

144

Saddle
Pad saddle made from tanned skin stuffed with
grass or hair. Transverse panel of tanned,
smoked skin conceals girth tabs on each side.
Girth straps of European tanned leather. Saddle
is decorated with porcupine-quill rosettes and
lozenges in band, zigzag-band and simple line
techniques. Quilled edge-seams. Looped, quill-
wrapped thong fringes. Around saddle edges,
fringe strands are linked by transverse line of
sinew strung with white beads. Quill colours are
red, blue, white, yellow and green. Sewn with
sinew.
L. 49 cm
Blackfoot type, c. 1840

*Collected by the Earl of Caledon in 1841–42. (James
Du Près, the third Earl of Caledon, of Tyrone, Ireland,
was in Canada between March 1841 and November
1842 while a captain of the Coldstream Guards.)*
NMM V–B–424

45

Crupper

Base of rawhide covered and extended by
tanned skin. Overlay of red stroud bound with
green woollen cloth, with green wool and beige
silk appliqués and outline of white beads. Large
quilled rosettes worked in band and simple line
techniques, outlined with deep turquoise-blue
pony beads, with tassels of quill-wrapped
thongs, metal cones and yellow wool attached at
centres. Long, fine thong fringes, each quill-
wrapped and ending in a red or yellow wool
tassel, linked with transverse sinew line strung
with blue pony beads. Quill colours are blue,
orange, brown, yellow, green and white.
w/o loop 58.5 cm
Northeastern Plains type, c. 1840

Meyer Collection; originally collected by Ehrentraut,
put in a museum by 1852.
MM V-X-393

146

Gun Case
Made from tanned, smoked skin, with appliqués
of tanned, unsmoked skin decorated with porcupine quillwork in zigzag-band technique,
painted blue-black rectangles and dots, red
and green woollen cloth, and tassels of red,
purple, yellow and white horsehair. Fringes of
unsmoked skin, quill-wrapped at top and joined
by transverse sinew line strung with bright-blue
beads. At barrel end, seam is covered by bright-
blue and deep-red beads. Skin edges are
notched. Sinew-sewn.
L. 145 cm
Sioux type, c. 1880

Collected at Lake Manitoba between 1875 and 1890
NMM V-E-295

147

Wampum Belt
Warp of fine thongs, weft of vegetable fibre
strung with purple and white shell beads. Beads
are irregular in size and shape.
L. w/o fringe 121.5 cm
Eastern Great Lakes, c. 1780

*Speyer Collection; formerly in the collection of Sir John
Caldwell (see No. 21).*
NMM III-X-253

148

Garters
Woven beadwork, on woollen yarn foundation.
Beads threaded on vegetable-fibre twine. Yarn
colours are light and dark brown and dull green.
Black and white pony beads are used.
L. beaded portion 21.5 cm
Central Algonkians or Eastern Plains, 1820

*Speyer Collection; formerly in the collection of the Earl
of Warwick, Warwick Castle.*
NMM III–X–240

150

149

Pouch with Carrying Strap
Finger-woven in olive-green woollen yarn.
White pony beads are interwoven to create a
diamond pattern on front and zigzag lines on
back. Top edges bound with discoloured silk
and edged with white beads. Porcupine-quill
appliqué in two-quill diamond technique on
tanned-skin transverse band. Tassels of metal
cones and red hair.
Carrying strap of two finger-woven bands,
joined at shoulder, in dull-red and olive-green
woollen yarns, with borders in black. White
beads interwoven in zigzag line down edges.
Warp ends braided and quill-wrapped.
L. w/o fringe 120 cm
Great Lakes, late eighteenth century

Speyer Collection; formerly in the Greatorex Collection,
Whitechapel Museum, London, and later in the James
Hooper Collection, England.
NMM III-X-263

Garter Pendant
Tightly finger-woven of hard-textured woollen
yarns. Black with red borders; white beads interwoven in geometric motifs and used for edging.
One end bound with yellow silk ribbon; the
other has fringe of braided warp-strands, each
quill-wrapped and strung at end with metal
cone and orange hair. Single eagle feather
attached by thong to sash: it is inserted into a
metal cone at quill end, and secured to it is a
wooden splint, quill-wrapped and decorated
with small red feathers.
L. w/o fringe 40.5 cm
Eastern Great Lakes, late eighteenth century

Speyer Collection
NMM III-X-258

151

Sash

Finger-woven of green woollen yarn, with
pattern in pale-blue and interwoven white beads.
At intervals down length, warp strands are
brought together and quill-wrapped; lines of
white beads strung crosswise between strands
separate colour blocks. At ends, fringes are
quill-wrapped and threaded with metal cones.
L. w/o fringe 120 cm
Eastern Great Lakes, late eighteenth century

*Speyer Collection; formerly in the collection of Captain
Alexander Hood, Royal Navy (d. 1796), a lieutenant
under Captain James Cook.*
NMM III–X–254

152

Pouch
Made of blue and black stroud lined with
printed beige cotton. Inside divider of brown
cloth. Edges bound with blue woollen tape.
Beads attached to front in overlay stitch.
Carrying strap of tanned, smoked skin. Black
plastic button.
L. w/o strap 21 cm
Naskapi, c. 1910

*Collected by E. Sapir at Pointe-Bleue, Quebec, in 1911.
Acquired from Louis Clairie, who had received it from
a Naskapi woman.*
NMM III–B–6

153

Pipe Bag with Cleaner
Made from tanned, smoked skin decorated with
white and deep-turquoise glass beads strung on
sinew and attached by lazy stitch. At base of bag
are quill-wrapped rawhide strips with fringes of
metal cones strung on fine rawhide thongs.
Pipe cleaner is a pointed wooden stick, which is
attached to a thong passed through the upper
front of the bag, its free ends strung with metal
cones. Sinew-sewn.
L. w. fringe 45 cm
Blackfoot type, early nineteenth century

Speyer Collection
NMM V–B–423

154

Coat
Made from sealskin in European cut. Edges are
bound with beaver. Appliqués of tanned, black-
dyed skin with floral designs in moose hair;
some appliqués edged with red silk. Insets in
contrasting white fur, representing head of pipe-
smoking Indian, tomahawk and beaver. Coat
lined with red silk brocade. Sewn with sinew
and vegetable-fibre twine. Moose-hair colours
are orange, blue, white, mauve and pink.
L. 103 cm
Huron, c. 1845

Speyer Collection; acquired from a dealer.
NMM III–H–424

155

Moccasins (colour plate, p. 58)
Made from black-dyed, tanned skin decorated
with moose-hair appliqué in oversewn-line
technique. Upright ankle-flaps have binding of
pink silk ribbon. Sewn with cotton thread.
Moose-hair colours are orange, white, pale blue,
and beige.
L. 24 cm
Huron type, 1840s

Speyer Collection; formerly in the collection of Sir
Charles Lyell. (Lyell, 1797–1875, was in Nova Scotia
in 1841, and again in North America in 1845.)
NMM III–H–427

156

Container
Made in two pieces, one of which slides over the
liner of the other. Both pieces consist of two
layers of birch bark. Moose-hair embroidery in
floral designs, with gradations of colour. Edges
covered with white moose hair, stitched at right
angles with brown cotton thread. Moose-hair
colours are green, yellow, white and orange.
9.5 cm L. × 6.5 W. × 2 D.
Huron type, c. 1850

Speyer Collection; acquired from a dealer in Brussels.
NMM III-H-436

157

Cradleboard
Of wood; bow and footrest attached with
thongs. Notching and openwork decoration
along top of board. Wood has been blackened
with a hot file, and has shallow engraved
designs. Painted designs in dark blue and purple
on back and, probably representing a turtle, on
underside of footrest. Thongs laced through
holes on sides. "Alex Fraser, Caledonia" written
in pencil on back.
L. 64 cm
Iroquois (Mohawk?) type, before 1860

*Speyer Collection; previously acquired by the Royal
Scottish Museum in 1860.*
NMM III-I-1328

158

Man's Coat (colour plate, p. 58)
Made from tanned skin. Flared skirt below high
waistline, with metal hook-and-eye closure from
neck to waist. Upstanding collar and full-length
sleeves with deep cuffs. Ermine trim down front
and around collar and cuffs. Short cut-skin
fringe added around bottom, with individual
strands quill-wrapped for about half their
length. Quill-wrapped thongs, netted quillwork,
and free-hanging skin fringe at shoulder and,
without netted technique, at centre back.
Delicate stylized floral patterns in quills applied
in zigzag-band, simple line, and sawtooth
techniques. Main seams quilled in sawtooth
technique. Quill colours are red, white, blue and
black.
L. 107 cm
Sioux–Métis type, c. 1840

Acquired from a dealer in New York in 1971
NMM V–E–294

159

Bag
Multicoloured beaded motifs of stylized floral
sprays worked on black wool broadcloth, with
woven beaded panel attached across lower edge.
Fringe formed by beads threaded on each warp
end and terminating in maroon wool tassels. Bag
is lined with pink cotton, edges bound with
dark-red silk ribbon. White bead edging. Sinew
and cotton thread used in beading.
L. w/o fringe 34 cm
Red River Métis type, second half of nineteenth century

Acquired from Mrs. R. C. Wilson, Ottawa; collected
by her father, Edward Prince, presumably during his
service as Commissioner and General Inspector of
Fisheries, 1893–1926.
NMM V–Z–2

160

Leggings
Made from blue wool broadcloth, with slit and
lower edge bound with blue cotton sateen and
edged with white beads. White and a few red
and blue beads attached by overlay stitch in
stylized floral border around lower edge.
L. 43 cm
Iroquois (Cayuga), before 1912

Collected by F. W. Waugh from Mrs. Mary Jacobs at
the Six Nations Reserve, Brant County, Ontario, in
1913
NMM III–I–909

1

ash

ightly finger-woven of hard-textured woollen
rns. Main colour is red, with grey-green
order on both sides and red selvages. Small
hite beads interwoven in geometric design.
eaded edging. Fringes twisted and knotted,
en braided for a length of 8 cm.
w/o fringe 78.5 cm
oquois, before 1845

*cquired in 1908 from D. H. Price. Given by Chief
imham to Richard Martin about 1845.*
MM III-I-322

162

Cradleboard
Made of wood, with bow secured by rawhide
thong. Back (illustrated) is elaborately carved
and painted with birds and floral designs;
designs are also painted on underside of footrest
(flowers) and top of front (bird and tree). Carved
bow. Colours are blue-black, red and green.
L. 79.5 cm
Iroquois, second half of nineteenth century

Collected at Oka, Quebec, in 1929
NMM III-I-1087

163

Mittens
Made from tanned, black-dyed skin, the backs
decorated with moose-hair appliqué in
oversewn-line technique. Moose-hair colours
are orange, pink, white, beige and blue. Sewn
with cotton thread.
L. 25 cm
Huron type, c. 1840

Collected by the Earl of Caledon in 1841–42
(see No. 144)
NMM III–H–408

164

Moccasins
Made from tanned, black-dyed skin decorated
with moose-hair appliqué in oversewn-line
technique. Compact fringe of red-dyed hair and
metal cones. Sewn with vegetable-fibre twine.
Moose-hair colours are orange, white, blue and
green.
L. 26.5 cm
Huron type, before 1829

Speyer Collection; formerly in the collection of the Duke
of Gotha.
NMM III–H–425

166

Box
Made from two layers of birch bark and
decorated with moose-hair embroidery. Hinged
lid. Edged with white moose hair (around
bottom with shredded grass), which is stitched at
right angles with brown cotton thread or
shredded plant fibre. Moose-hair colours are
green, orange, beige and white.
11.5 cm L. × 8 W. × 5 D.
Huron type, c. 1850

Speyer Collection
NMM III-H-438

5

ouch
ade from sealskin, with caribou lower leg
wn to front. Edges trimmed with notched red
oollen cloth. Two small pockets of tanned,
ack-dyed skin sewn to front and decorated
ith moose-hair appliqué in orange, white and
ue. Row of holes beneath top edge of pouch,
ch covered with copper disc. Closure consists
an eyed piece of tanned skin buttoned over a
in-covered wooden toggle. Suspension loop of
nned, smoked skin.
41 cm
uron type, 1843

eyer Collection
MM III-H-437

167

Basket
Woven from wooden splints in chequer weave
on base and upper and lower circumferences
and in wicker weave around sides. Exterior
decorated with stamped designs in green, yellow
and pale orange.
Diam. 28 cm
Iroquois type, 1850

Acquired in 1974; collected in the lower Ottawa
Valley, Ontario.
NMM III-I-1329

168

Container
Made from birch bark, seamed with split spruce-root. Lid fits inside basket rim, which is bound with roots. Thong handle. Decorated with floral designs achieved by scraping away the dark inner bark, which is to the exterior of the container, to expose the lighter bark beneath.
L. 17.8 cm
Algonkin, before 1913

Collected by F. G. Speck at Mattawa, Ontario, in 1913
NMM III-L-191

169

Container
Made of a double layer of birch bark, with edges covered with sweet grass bound with black cotton thread. Lid and sides decorated with white porcupine quillwork, the thistle motif predominating. Dated "Aug. 1914" on base.
Diam. 15 cm; H. 12 cm
Ojibwa, 1914

Acquired in 1960; collected by A. Acres, of Parry Sound, Ontario.
NMM III-G-431

170

Neckwear
Rectangle of teal-blue velvet backed with pink
cotton and edged with red and purple silk
ribbon. Outline beading in two rows of red glass
beads represents horned human figure. Beads
are attached by overlay stitch with cotton
thread. Red ribbon ties. Type of neckwear worn
in Medicine Lodge rituals.
H. 27 cm
Ojibwa type, early twentieth century

Acquired from a dealer in New York in 1974
NMM III-G-836

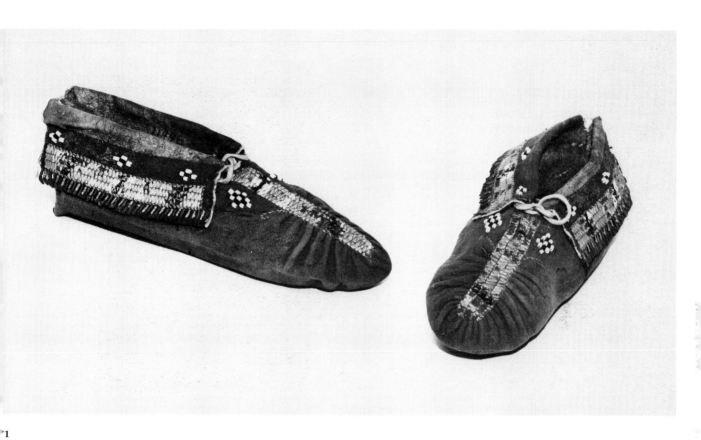

1

Moccasins
Made from tanned, black-dyed skin decorated
with porcupine quills in zigzag-band and simple
line techniques. Ankle-flap edges are cut into
short fringe, which is quill-wrapped. Beaded
diamond patterns in cylindrical white and black
glass beads. Sinew-sewn. Quill colours are
orange, black and white.
25.5 cm
Menomini(?), late eighteenth century

*Speyer Collection; formerly in the collection of the Duke
of Gotha.*
IMM III–N–32

173

Garter Pendant
Tightly finger-woven of hard-textured woollen
yarns. Main panel is green, with faded maroon
borders and green selvage. White beads interwoven in geometric pattern. One end bound
with red wool and bead-edged; at other end,
fringe is of braided warp-strands, quill-wrapped
(white, black and red) and strung with tin cones
and red wool tassels at ends.
L. w/o fringe 45 cm
Eastern Great Lakes, c. 1780

*Speyer Collection; formerly in the collection of Sir John
Caldwell (see No. 21).*
NMM III-X-255

172

Pouch
Made of cotton cloth, with bead-woven panel on
front terminating in tab fringe, each tab with
two tassels of red and black wool. Back, above
pocket, of black velvet with floral spray of
multicoloured beads attached by overlay stitch.
Sides bound with red worsted tape and
decorated with green ribbon appliqué and lines
of yellow and transparent milky-blue beads.
Bead-woven shoulder strap backed by natural
canvas and checked cotton. Beaded designs are
similar, but not identical, down either side, and
colour combinations are different. Beaded with
cotton thread.
L. pouch w/o fringe 44 cm; L. strap 90 cm
Ojibwa type, early twentieth century

Acquired from a dealer in New York in 1973
NMM III-G-837

174

Man's Shirt
Made of dark-red felt, with applied panels of
beaded black velvet. Front and back in one
piece, with slightly shaped armholes, round
neck, and short vertical front opening. Panels
are edged with blue worsted tape, and in
addition the front yoke is outlined with large
white beads. All panels are decorated with
stylized floral sprays with white stems and multicoloured blossoms. Beaded with cotton thread.
L. 64 cm
Ojibwa, early twentieth century

Collected by A. B. Reagan, at the Bois Fort Reservation, northern Minnesota, in 1913
NMM III-G-164

175

Pouch
Made from tanned, smoked skin decorated with porcupine quills in zigzag-band technique in orange, turquoise, black and white. Edges originally bound with red silk ribbon; pocket top edged with white glass beads. Fringe (now fragmentary) of quill-wrapped thongs with tassels of metal cones and orange hair attached in bottom seam. Sewn with cotton thread and sinew.
L. w/o fringe 29 cm
Menomini, before 1850

Speyer Collection; formerly in the Greatorex Collection, Whitechapel Museum, London; later in the James Hooper Collection, England.
NMM III-N-33

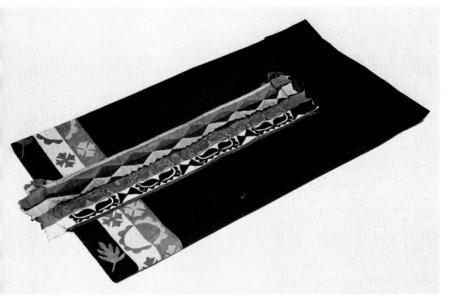

176

Woman's Skirt
Black wool broadcloth with ribbon appliqué
around hem and down unseamed front opening.
Feather stitching around some appliqués.
Ribbon appliqué is backed with printed cottons.
Ribbons are cut and folded, and sewn with silk
thread.
L. 120 cm
Menomini, c. 1900

Collected by A. B. Skinner in 1913
NMM III–N–29

177

Pouch
Made from hard-textured woollen yarns, tightly
finger-woven. Natural dyes have been used;
main colour is deep ochre-red, with a yellow
transverse band on front and back produced by
either discharge- or resist-dye technique. Brown
border. White beads interwoven to produce
diamond pattern on front, vertical zigzag lines
on back. Top back, above pocket, and
downturned flap at pocket top are of tanned
skin decorated with three lanes of porcupine
quills, in zigzag-band technique, dyed orange,
white and black. Fringe of quill-wrapped thongs,
metal cones, and red-dyed hair. Sewn with
sinew and cotton thread.
L. w/o fringe 20 cm
Great Lakes, eighteenth century

Speyer Collection; formerly in the collection of the Earl
of Warwick, Warwick Castle.
NMM III–X–256

178

Sash
Tightly finger-woven from hard-textured olive-green woollen yarn, with small white beads interwoven in geometric pattern. Long warp ends are quill-wrapped, forming fringe, each strand strung with a metal cone and tassel of red-dyed hair at end. Near sash ends, glass imitations of wampum beads are strung between fringe strands. Quill colours are white, red and greenish blue.
L. w/o fringe 111 cm
Eastern Great Lakes, eighteenth century

Speyer Collection; formerly in the Greatorex Collection, Whitechapel Museum, London. Later in the James Hooper Collection, England.
NMM III-X-257

179

Pipe
Wooden stem carved to create twisted effect. Edges burn-marked. Pipe bowl of red pipestone (catlinite) with lead inlay. Leaf pattern inlaid on one side of lower bowl, four arrows on the other.
L. bowl 18 cm; L. pipe stem 83 cm
Sioux, c. 1860

Speyer Collection; formerly in the James Hooper Collection, England.
NMM V-E-276

180

Man's Hood
Made of napped dark-blue stroud, lined with
red bandanna. All edges originally trimmed with
blue and white beads. Around the front and the
lower edge are three bands of floral motifs in
multicoloured beads, separated by lines of
maroon ribbon edged with white beads. Red and
blue stroud tuft at top. Bead colours are white,
rose, medium blue, green and clear. Sewn with
sinew and cotton and silk thread.
H. 51 cm
*Tête-de-Boule (James Bay Cree type), late nineteenth
century*

*Collected by Rev. Henry Stuart at La Tuque, Quebec,
about 1890*
NMM III-C-512

181

Beaded Band
Pattern of multicoloured cut beads on white
ground. Worked on strips of caribou skin,
stained red, with weft of black cotton thread.
L. 54.5 cm
Naskapi, 1920s

Collected by Richard White at Nain, Labrador,
in 1929
NMM III–B–41

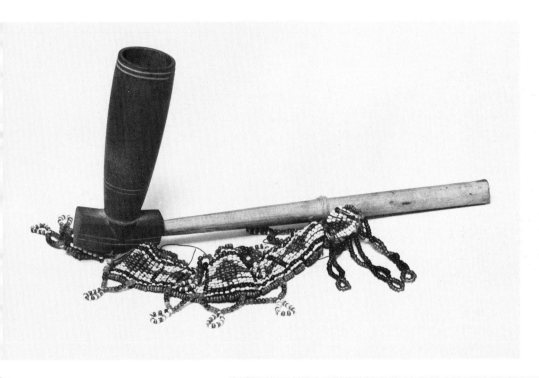

pe
wl of grey-green soapstone decorated with
cised lines. Wooden stem tapered toward
wl. Bowl and stem are linked by strip of
oven beadwork in red, white, and two shades
blue glass beads on warp of cotton thread.
bowl 8.6 cm; L. stem 14.6 cm
ampy Cree, 1915

llected by E. Renouf, a Hudson's Bay Co. employee,
Great Whale River, Quebec, in 1915
MM III-D-28

183

Gloves (colour plate, p. 59)
Gauntlets made from tanned, smoked skin and
trimmed with black fur. Wrists are lined with
burgundy velvet, hands with flannelette. Sewn
with cotton thread and sinew. Backs decorated
with multicoloured silk embroidery.
L. 43 cm
Cree–Métis type, late nineteenth century

Acquired from a dealer in New York in 1972
NMM III-D-389

184

Child's Jacket
Of heavy cotton, solidly beaded in overlay
stitch. Red wool and cotton binding around
edges; fringes of cut skin. Two charms attached
at neck back: an umbilical-cord amulet, solidly
beaded, with three pairs of brass-bead stringers;
and an oval beaded ring with three pairs of
bead-edged pendant skin strips strung with
brass cones. Bead colours are blue, green, gold,
rose and ochre against a white background. A
few faceted silver-coloured metal beads are
used. Sewn with cotton thread throughout.
L. 33 cm
Plains Ojibwa type, c. 1914

*Acquired from Mrs. Charles Cundy, who obtained it
in northern Saskatchewan, c. 1914. The jacket was
presented to Mr. Cundy after he had saved the life of a
chief's son. It had belonged to the boy.*
NMM V–F–105

85

Man's Hood

Made from red stroud decorated with green,
pink and blue ribbon-appliqué and white beads
attached by overlay stitch. On each side is a
beaded circle divided into quarters by beaded
lines. Sewn and beaded with cotton thread.
L. 67 cm
Minnesota Ojibwa, before 1850

*Speyer Collection; formerly in the collection of
Göttingen University, West Germany; previously
owned by Hermann Domeier, who acquired it in
Europe in about 1852.*
NMM III–G–838

186

Bag

Made of red stroud, with ribbon and white bead
edging. Outline design on one side in bright-
blue seed beads and chain stitch in yellow and
black silk. On both sides, near top, are two discs
of blue flannel outlined in white beads, with
beaded tassel fringes. Narrow finger-woven ties
in red, green and white yarns cross inside of bag
and are threaded through discs on back. Woven
beadwork panel at bottom, with symmetrical
geometric pattern in coloured beads against a
white background. Warp ends of panel are
threaded with beads to form a fringe, each end
terminating in a red wool tassel. Bag is lined
with striped cotton.
L. 25.5 cm; panel 11 cm
Red River Métis type, nineteenth century

*Acquired from Mrs. T. P. Foran, Ottawa, in 1935.
Formerly owned by Rev. George A. Hay, Nova Scotia,
who died in 1873.*
NMM V–Z–3

187

Bag
Made of black wool broadcloth, bound with
blue silk ribbon. White bead edging and multicoloured floral beadwork on both sides in
overlay-stitch technique. Ends of tabs finished
with double tassels of large faceted beads ending
in tufts of coloured wool. Lined with striped
cotton print. Twisted red and black wool
carrying cord secured to back with brass
buttons. Sewn with sinew and cotton thread.
L. 32 cm
Northwest Territories Métis type, c. 1840–70

*Acquired in 1914 from S. H. Harris, who obtained it
about 1870. (Harris was a fur broker to the Hudson's
Bay Co. at their London office. Specimens were sent to
him there from Canada.)*
NMM VI-Z-196

188

Knife and Sheath (colour plate, p. 60)
Sheath of tanned, unsmoked (white) skin with
broad band of woven porcupine quillwork
attached at top front. Long thong fringes, looped
and quill-wrapped, are attached at top and
bottom of one side; shorter similar fringes along
bottom of quill-woven band. There are white
glass beads down sides of band and strung
between strands of the long fringes. Sheath front
is decorated with quills in zigzag-band,
sawtooth, and simple line techniques. Single-
quill edging. Quill-wrapped suspension loop.
Birch-bark liner. Sinew-sewn. Quill colours are
red, blue, white, and smaller amounts of green
and yellow.
Knife has broad, double-edged iron blade, and
black bone handle with circular inlays of brass
and white bone.
L. sheath 29.5 cm; L. knife 30.5 cm
Red River Métis type, c. 1840

Collected by the Earl of Caledon in 1841–42
(see No. 144)
NMM V-Z-4

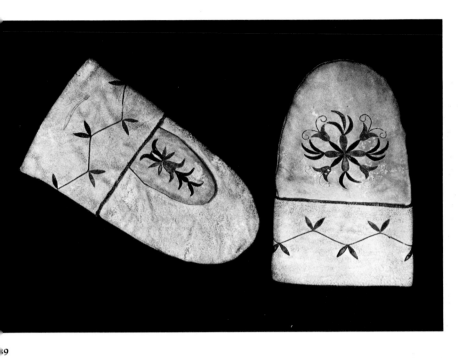

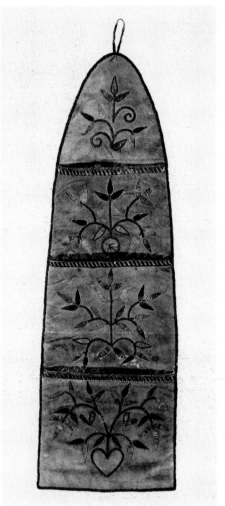

9

Mittens

Made of tanned, unsmoked skin decorated with
delicate quilled floral and leaf patterns on
thumb, back of hand, and around cuff. Quills
are applied in four techniques: zigzag band,
simple line, edging, and oversewn piping.
Colours are blue (two shades), red, and white.
Sewn with sinew.

24 cm
Red River Métis type, c. 1840

Collected by the Earl of Caledon in 1841–42
(see No. 144)
NMM V–Z–1

190

Roll-up Bag
Made from tanned, unsmoked skin, with three
pockets lined with unbleached cotton.
Decorated with porcupine-quill appliqué in
band, sawtooth, simple line, and zigzag-band
techniques. One-quill edging. Quill-wrapped
suspension loop at top. Quill colours are red,
blue, purple, yellow, green and white. Sewn
with cotton thread and sinew. Top originally
backed with striped cotton.
L. 41 cm
Plains Cree, 1830–40

*Speyer Collection; formerly in the collection of Captain
Fuller. An old label reads: "A Cree Indian's Woman
Sinew Pouch ornamented with stained Porcupine Quills
from the Plains on the Banks of the Saskatchewan
River, North America".*
NMM V–A–408

191

Mittens
Made from tanned, smoked skin, with deep cuff
of smoked skin originally trimmed with fur.
Porcupine-quill appliqué in simple line and
zigzag-band techniques. Quill colours are green,
blue, red, yellow, white, and a small amount of
purple and brown. Bird-quill piping along
thumb seam. Sewn with cotton thread and
sinew.
L. 26 cm
Eastern Sioux type, c. 1840

Speyer Collection
NMM V-E-293

Paintings, Drawings and Prints Depicting the Period

Note The National Museum of Man
appreciates the generosity of the
owners of the original works of art
(marked with an asterisk) in making
them available for exhibition in Ottawa.
However, a few of these works could
not be retained for the entire cross-
Canada tour; in such cases,
reproductions have been supplied for
display in other centres. Dimensions
throughout are height × width.

Cornelius Krieghoff
Officer's Trophy Room. 1846
Oil on canvas, 44.5 × 63.5 cm

Courtesy Canadiana Department, Royal Ontario
Museum, Toronto

*Artist unknown
Soldiering with the King's, 1780. (Sir John
Caldwell, British officer, in Eastern Great Lakes
Indian dress of the 1780s. Reproduced in colour
on the cover.)
Oil on canvas, 127.0 × 101.6 cm

*Courtesy King's Regiment Collection, Merseyside
County Museums, Liverpool, England*

*George Catlin
Wi-Jun-Jon, the Pigeon's Egg Head. 1844
Hand-coloured lithograph, 59.7 × 47.1 cm

Courtesy Amon Carter Museum, Fort Worth, Texas

G. Lazare and L. Parker
The Villagers Assemble. (Reconstruction of a village of long houses like those used by the Huron and Iroquois.) 1969
Mixed media, 63.5 × 72.6 cm

Courtesy Lazare and Parker Studio, Toronto

F. A. Verner
Lake of the Woods. (A typical camp scene in the Northeastern Forest.) 1873
Graphite and watercolour, 14.2 × 30.0 cm

Courtesy National Gallery of Canada, Ottawa

Charles M. Russell
Indian Hunters Return. (A winter camp of the
Northern Plains Indians.) 1900
Oil on canvas, 61.0 × 91.4 cm

*Courtesy Mackay Collection, Montana Historical
Society, Helena*

*Charles M. Russell
The Picture Robe. (A Plains Indian painting his war record on skin.) 1899
Ink on paper, 27.3 × 37.2 cm

Courtesy Amon Carter Museum, Fort Worth, Texas

*Charles M. Russell
The Silk Robe. (Scraping a fresh skin staked out on the ground.) c. 1890
Oil on canvas, 70.2 × 99.3 cm

Courtesy Amon Carter Museum, Fort Worth, Texas

*After Edward Chatfield
**Nicholas Vincent Isawanhoni, a Huron Chief,
Holding a Wampum Belt.** 1825
Hand-coloured lithograph, 45.8 × 33.1 cm

Courtesy Public Archives of Canada, Ottawa

*After Carl Bodmer
Assiniboin Indians. 1839
Aquatint, 60.7 × 43.9 cm

*Courtesy Northern Natural Gas Company Collection,
Joslyn Art Museum, Omaha, Nebr.*

George Catlin
**Medicine Man Performing His Mysteries over
a Dying Man.** (Blackfoot.) 1832
Oil on canvas, 73.7 × 61.0 cm

*Courtesy National Collection of Fine Arts, Smithsonian
Institution, Washington, D.C.*

George Catlin
Old Bear, a Medicine Man. (A Mandan priest
holding the sacred calumet stems.) 1832
Oil on canvas, 73.7 × 61.0 cm

*Courtesy National Collection of Fine Arts, Smithsonian
Institution, Washington, D.C.*

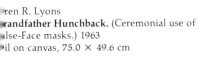

ren R. Lyons
randfather Hunchback. (Ceremonial use of
lse-Face masks.) 1963
il on canvas, 75.0 × 49.6 cm

urtesy of the artist

*Paul Kane
A Cree from Fort Carlton. 1846
Watercolour over pencil, 22.9 × 14.1 cm

*Courtesy Ethnology Department, Royal Ontario
Museum, Toronto*

Paul Kane
Mani-Tow-Wa-Bay (He-Devil), Ojibway Chief.
1846
Oil on paper, 29.6 × 22.0 cm

Courtesy Glenbow-Alberta Institute, Calgary

*After Carl Bodmer
Dakota Woman and Assiniboin Girl. 1830s
Aquatint, 60.7 × 43.9 cm

*Courtesy Northern Natural Gas Company Collection,
Joslyn Art Museum, Omaha, Nebr.*

'Paul Kane
Cun-Ne-Wa-Bum ("One That Looks at the Stars", a Half-Breed Cree Beauty at Fort Edmonton). 1846
Oil on canvas, 63.5 × 50.9 cm

Courtesy Ethnology Department, Royal Ontario Museum, Toronto

George Catlin
he Six (Shacopay), **Chief of the Plains Ojibwa.**
832
Oil on canvas, 73.7 × 61.0 cm

Courtesy National Collection of Fine Arts, Smithsonian
Institution, Washington, D.C.

*Paul Kane
**Kitchie-Ogi-Maw (the Great Chief of the
Menominee Indians at Fox River).** 1845
Oil on canvas, 71.1 × 63.5 cm

*Courtesy Ethnology Department, Royal Ontario
Museum, Toronto*

Peter Rindisbacher
Captain W. Andrew Bulger Saying Farewell at Fort MacKay, Prairie du Chien, Wisconsin, 1815. (Showing a group of Ojibwa Indians.)
1823
Ink and watercolour, 35.6 × 60.7 cm

Courtesy Amon Carter Museum, Fort Worth, Texas

George Romney
Portrait of Joseph Brant. (Thayendanegea, Mohawk-Iroquois war chief.) c. 1776
Oil on canvas, 127.0 × 101.6 cm

Courtesy National Gallery of Canada, Ottawa

*Peter Rindisbacher
Man and Two Women. (Red River Métis; sketch
for his painting *A Halfcast and His Two
Wives.*) c. 1825–26
Pencil, 16.5 × 19.0 cm

Courtesy Glenbow-Alberta Institute, Calgary

Zacharie Vincent
Vincent, Zacharie (Telariolin). (Huron Indian
chief; self-portrait.) c. 1850
Oil on paper, 73.7 × 54.7 cm

Courtesy Château de Ramezay Museum, Montreal

*Sir Joshua Jebb
Two Ottawa Chiefs. c. 1813–20
Watercolour, 24.2 × 29.3 cm

Courtesy Peabody Museum of Archaeology and Ethnology, Cambridge, Mass.

*After H. D. Thielcke
The Presentation of a Newly-elected Chief of the Huron Tribe, Canada. (Lorette, Quebec.) 1841
Hand-coloured lithograph, 48.0 × 39.2 cm

Courtesy McCord Museum, Montreal

*Louis-Joseph Dulongpré
Mère Thérèse Geneviève Coutlée. (A Grey Nun
busy with embroidery.) c. 1800
Oil on canvas, 91.4 × 61.0 cm

Courtesy Sœurs Grises de Montréal

*Peter Rindisbacher
A Cree Hunter and His Family at Fort York:
1821
Ink and watercolour, 16.0 × 21.9 cm

Courtesy Public Archives of Canada, Ottawa

Peter Rindisbacher
An Indian Scalp Dance. (Southern Manitoba.)
1820s
Ink and watercolour, 22.3 × 27.4 cm

Courtesy Hudson's Bay Company, Winnipeg

George Catlin
Ju-Ah-Kis-Gaw (Ojibwa Woman with Child in Cradle). 1834
Oil on canvas, 73.7 × 61.0 cm

Courtesy National Collection of Fine Arts, Smithsonian Institution, Washington, D.C.

Paul Kane
François Lucie, Cree-Métis Guide. 1846
Oil on paper, 27.7 × 22.3 cm

Courtesy Stark Museum of Art, Orange, Texas

*Irving Couse
The Chant. (Shows use of hand drum.) n. d.
Oil on canvas, 61.6 × 74.0 cm

Courtesy Amon Carter Museum, Fort Worth, Texas

*Cornelius Krieghoff
The Basket Seller. (St. Lawrence Valley.) c. 1850
Oil on cardboard, 24.8 × 19.0 cm

Courtesy Art Gallery of Ontario, Toronto (Gift from the Fund of the T. Eaton Co. Ltd. for Canadian Works of Art, 1951)

*Paul Kane
Indian Encampment on Lake Huron. c. 1845–50
Oil on canvas, 48.4 × 73.7 cm

Courtesy Art Gallery of Ontario, Toronto

After Edward Chatfield
**Three Chiefs of the Huron Indians, Residing at
La Jeune Lorette, near Quebec.** 1825
Hand-coloured lithograph, 48.4 × 38.8 cm

Courtesy Public Archives of Canada, Ottawa

*Paul Kane
Blackfoot Chief and Subordinates. (Big Snake
recounting his exploits.) 1851–56
Oil on canvas, 63.5 × 76.2 cm

Courtesy National Gallery of Canada, Ottawa

Peter Rindisbacher
Indian Women in Tent. 1820s
Watercolour, 19.2 × 20.4 cm

*Courtesy West Point Museum, United States Military
Academy, West Point, N.Y.*

After C. B. King
Okee-Maakee-Quid, Chippeway Chief.
(Reproduced from T. L. McKenney and James
Hall, *The History of the Indian Tribes of North
America,* vol. 1 [Philadelphia, 1836].)
Lithograph, 52 × 36 cm

Courtesy Glenbow-Alberta Institute, Calgary

Some Suggestions for Further Reading

American Indian Art: Form and Tradition. Minneapolis, Minn.: Walker Art Center, 1972.

The Art of the Great Lakes Indians. Flint, Mich.: Flint Institute of Arts, 1973.

The Athapaskans: Strangers of the North. Ottawa: National Museum of Man, National Museums of Canada, 1974.

Barbeau, Marius. *Assomption Sash.* National Museum of Canada Bulletin 93. Ottawa, [1937?].

———. *Indian Days on the Western Prairies.* National Museum of Canada Bulletin 163. Ottawa, 1960.

Benndorf, Helge, and Arthur Speyer. *Indianer Nordamerikas, 1760–1860.* Offenbach am Main, West Germany: Deutsches Ledermuseum, Deutsches Schuhmuseum, 1968.

Brasser, Ted J. "Group Identification along a Moving Frontier". *Verhandlungen des 38 Internationalen Amerikanistenkongresses.* Band 2. Munich: Renner, 1970, pp. 261–65.

Conn, R. *Robes of White Shell and Sunrise.* Denver, Colo.: Denver Art Museum, 1975.

Densmore, F. *Chippewa Customs.* Edited by Elliott Coues. Bureau of American Ethnology Bulletin 86. Washington, D.C., 1929.

Ewers, J. C. *Plains Indian Painting.* Stanford, Calif.: Stanford University Press, 1939.

———. *Blackfeet Crafts.* U. S. Office of Indian Affairs, Indian Handcrafts 9. Lawrence, Kans.: U.S. Indian Service, 1945.

Feder, Norman. *Art of the Eastern Plains Indians.* Brooklyn, N.Y.: Brooklyn Museum, 1964.

———. *American Indian Art.* New York: Abrams, 1971.

Feest, Christian F. *Indianer Nordamerikas.* Vienna: Museum Für Völkerkunde, 1968.

Fenton, William N. "Masked Medicine Societies of the Iroquois". In *Smithsonian Institution, 14th Annual Report, 1940.* Washington, D.C., 1941, pp. 397–429.

———. *The Iroquois Eagle Dance, an Offshoot of the Calumet Dance. . . .* Bureau of American Ethnology Bulletin 156. Washington, D.C., 1953.

Henry, Alexander. *Travels and Adventures in Canada and the Indian Territories, between the years 1760 and 1766.* New ed. Edited, with notes, by James Bain. Edmonton, Alta.: Hurtig, [c. 1969].

——— and David Thompson. *The Manuscript Journals of Alexander Henry . . . and of David Thompson . . . 1799–1814.* 3 vols. Edited by Elliott Coues. New York: Harper, 1897.

Innis, H. A. *The Fur Trade in Canada.* Rev. ed. Toronto: University of Toronto Press, 1956.

Jenness, Diamond. *The Ojibwa Indians of Parry Island, Their Social and Religious Life.* National Museum of Canada Bulletin 78. Ottawa, 1935.

Krickeberg, W. *Altere Ethnographica aus Nordamerika.* . . . Baessler-Archiv, New Series, Band 2. Berlin: Reimer, 1954.

Kurz, Rudolph Friedrich. *Journal . . . 1846 to 1852.* Translated by Myrtis Jarrell; edited by J. N. B. Hewitt. Bureau of American Ethnology Bulletin 115. Washington, D.C., 1937.

Lyford, Carrie A. *Quill and Beadwork of the Western Sioux.* Edited by Willard W. Beatty. U.S. Office of Indian Affairs, Indian Handcrafts 1. Lawrence, Kans.: Haskell Institute, 1940.

————. *Iroquois Crafts.* Edited by Willard W. Beatty. U.S. Bureau of Indian Affairs, Indian Handcrafts 6. Lawrence, Kans.: Haskell Institute, 1945.

————. *The Crafts of the Ojibwa (Chippewa).* 2nd ed. Edited by Willard W. Beatty. U.S. Bureau of Indian Affairs, Indian Handcrafts 5. Lawrence, Kans.: Haskell Institute, 1953.

Marriott, A. "Ribbon Appliqué Work of North American Indians". *Oklahoma Anthropological Society Bulletin 6.* Norman, Okla., 1958, pp. 49–59.

Müller, W. *Die Religionen der Waldlandindianer Nordamerikas.* Berlin: Reimer, 1956.

Orchard, W. C. *The Technique of Porcupine-Quill Decoration among the North American Indians.* Contributions from the Museum 6 (1). New York: Museum of the American Indian, Heye Foundation, 1916.

————. *Beads and Beadwork of the American Indians.* Contributions from the Museum 11. New York: Museum of the American Indian, Heye Foundation, 1929.

Quimby, G. I. *Indian Life in the Upper Great Lakes, 11,000 B.C. to A.D. 1800.* Chicago: University of Chicago Press, 1960.

Ray, Arthur, Jr. *Indian Exploitation of the Forest-Grassland Transition Zone in Western Canada, 1650–1860.* Ph.D. dissertation, University of Wisconsin, 1971. Ann Arbor, Mich.: University Microfilms, 1975. (Published as *Indian in the Fur Trade: Their Role as Trappers, Hunters, and Middlemen in the Lands Southwest of Hudson Bay, 1660–1870.* Toronto: University of Toronto Press, [c. 1974].)

Ritzenthaler, R. E. *Iroquois False-Face Masks.* Milwaukee, Wis.: Milwaukee Public Museum, 1969.

Skinner, A. B. *Social Life and Ceremonial Bundles of the Menomini Indians.* Anthropological Papers of the American Museum of Natural History 13 (1). New York, 1913.

Speck, F. G. *Naskapi.* Norman, Okla.: University of Oklahoma Press, 1935.

————. *The Iroquois.* 2nd ed. Cranbrook Institute of Science Bulletin 23. Bloomfield Hills, Mich., 1955.

Speyer, Arthur. *See* Benndorf, Helge, and Arthur Speyer.

Turner, Geoffrey. *Hair Embroidery in Siberia and North America.* Pitt Rivers Museum, Occasional Paper on Technology 7. Oxford, England: At the University Press, 1955.

Turner, Lucien M. "Ethnology of the Ungava District, Hudson Bay Territory". In *Bureau of American Ethnology, 11th Annual Report, 1889–1890.* Washington, D.C., 1894, pp. 159–350.